Political Issues of Modern Britain
Editors: Bernard Crick and Patrick Seyd

The Politics of Economic Planning

ALAN BUDD

Fontana/Collins

Published by Fontana 1978
Copyright © Alan Budd 1978

Made and printed in Great Britain by
William Collins Sons & Co. Ltd, Glasgow

The Politics of Economic Planning is published in
hardback by Manchester University Press

To Susan

Contents

Editors' Preface

This new series aims to put into the hands of the intelligent general reader concise and authoritative accounts of the major issues of British politics today.

Writing on politics has often suffered from being either strident polemic or ephemeral journalism or else from being academic monographs too technical or theoretical for the general reader. This series hopes to fill an important gap – for it is more difficult to find reliable accounts of what happened ten or twenty years ago than fifty – by covering the issues which opinion polls and experts have judged to be the major issues of contemporary British politics.

We say 'issues' deliberately and not *problems*. Perhaps, indeed, beneath all these explicit issues, election slogans, public worries and press campaigns, there are fundamental and implicit economic and social problems. Theories, whether Marxist or capitalist, are not lacking to explain them all and to put them all in a 'correct theoretical perspective'. Our aim is more modest and precise: to remedy the lack of books that give accounts of those concerns which might reflect forces more fundamental, but will appear as concrete issues to ordinary people in everyday life. These books will be about politics and not political science.

Each book will cover three main topics: (i) a brief summary of the origins of the issue and fuller account of its history since the Second World War; (ii) an account of its institutional setting and of the pressure groups associated with the issues; and (iii) an account of what should be done and what is likely to happen. We ask each author to be as objective and as balanced as possible on the first two topics, but as polemical and as stimulating as he or she thinks fit in the third.

The series aims to achieve the same high standards of judgement but also of brevity that have been typical of the Fontana Modern Masters series. It aims to fulfil much the same function: both to be an introduction to the general reader and to be a way in which a specialist in one field can communicate with a specialist in another. If we may draw an analogy, we have briefed our authors to attempt that demanding but non-technical level of writing that is typical of the *Political Quarterly* at its best. Yet while the series is primarily intended for the general reader, students of history, politics, economics and social administration will find that the books fill a gap. They reflect a growing concern in the academic study of politics to look first at actual issues, rather than at institutions or methodologies.

If new editions are warranted, the complete books will, of course, be revised. But each time there is a reprint, we will ask the author to update the section on policy, on what is to be done. Thus each reprint will be topical while the edition places the issue in a deeper historical and institutional setting. We hope that this novel feature of the series will help it to be a contribution to what Walter Bagehot once hoped for from Parliamentary debates, 'the political education of mankind'. For that education seems at the moment so often to suffer from books which are a strange mixture of abstract theory and instant polemic. Issues need studying in an historical context if we are to act sensibly and effectively; and act we must.

Bernard Crick
Patrick Seyd

Author's Preface

This book might more accurately be entitled *The Economics of the Politics of Planning*. As an economist I have obeyed the doctrine of comparative advantage and have concentrated on the economic aspects of planning issues. I have tried to avoid writing a history of economic policy, but I believe that the politics of planning cannot be understood unless one also tries to understand the economic constraints within which policy operates. It is the failure to recognize these constraints that leads both to occasional attempts at planning and to their subsequent failure.

In his Preface to *A Treatise on Money* Keynes wrote,

> As I read through the page-proofs of this book I am acutely conscious of its defects. It has occupied me for several years, not free from other occupations, during which my ideas have been developing and changing, with the result that its parts are not all entirely harmonious with one another. The ideas with which I have finished up are widely different from those with which I began. The result is, I am afraid, that there is a good deal in this book which represents the process of getting rid of the ideas which I used to have and of finding my way to those which I now have.

While not claiming any other comparison with that great work, my experience in writing this book has been rather similar. I started it believing there was not enough economic planning in Britain and ended it believing there was too much. I would have found the task easier some years ago or some years hence. If any coherence emerges, this is largely due to the careful work of Patrick Seyd and Helen Fraser in commenting on earlier drafts. In the course of the development of my views I have learnt a great deal from conversations with friends and colleagues, especially Sam Aaronovitch, Michael Beenstock, Terry Burns, Patrick Minford and Henry Neuburger. Some of them will be pleased and some horrified by the views expressed in this book.

I am aware that in ending by supporting the market, I am leaving the company of many of the good and the great, and that I share my belief in markets with many who callously disregard their worst effects. But, as Adam Smith pointed out in *The Theory of Moral Sentiments*, it is dangerous to judge arguments according to the motives of those who propose them. (Harold Rose drew my attention to this reference.) In the end I find the liberal arguments convincing, and hope that some socialists who read this book will be led to reconsider the traditional hostility of the Labour Party to the market, and whether its objectives cannot best be achieved by less rather than more intervention.

I must thank the librarians of the London Business School and of the British Library of Political and Economic Science for their assistance. I am grateful to Sue Halfhide and to Helen Rothbarth for assistance with typing. During the period of writing this book, I was Williams and Glyn's Research Fellow at the London Business School, and I am grateful to them for their support.

My greatest debt of gratitude is to my wife Susan, who has encouraged me and made helpful comments and suggestions throughout. She has always been my most valuable critic and adviser, even if she remains a general sceptic about economics. As far as this book is concerned, she has seen positively final deadlines for completion come and go with tedious frequency and has patiently borne all the disruption it has caused. In a very busy life she even ended by doing most of the typing. I could not possibly have written it without her help.

Chapter 1: Introduction

British economic history since the Second World War has been dominated by a compromise between central planning at one end of the economic spectrum and a total reliance on market forces at the other. Neither one of the two extremes has been acceptable to British governments or their supporters, although there have been occasional shifts in policy towards something called planning, and shifts towards more liberal policies. The task of this book is to explain the ideas, events and interests which have produced the traditional attitudes to planning and the occasional lurches in policy towards it.

The matter is complicated by the many different definitions that 'planning' has been given. The beginning of planning in the United Kingdom has been dated from 1929 by one commentator,[1] from 1947 by another,[2] and from 1962 by a third.[3] To make matters yet more difficult, the word planning is often used as a slogan. There are times when everyone believes in planning and claim that they are doing it, while their opponents argue that it is not 'real' planning. This was true, for example, shortly before the Second World War. As Lord Robbins said then, ' "Planning" is the grand panacea of our age.'[4] There are also times when it falls into disrepute and everyone claims that they are doing something else. J. K. Galbraith remarked of the post-war period, 'For a public official to be called an economic planner was less serious than to be charged with communism or imaginative perversion, but reflected adversely nevertheless.'[5]

The shifts in meaning suggest we should distinguish between an absolutist and relativist history of economic planning. The first would take a specific definition and trace the history of that kind of planning. The second would study whatever happened to be called economic planning at the time. The first approach would be too broad or too narrow for our purposes. If, for example, we used the pre-war sense of planning, we might find ourselves writing the complete history of post-war economic management. If we used planning in its 1962–6 sense, there would be little to say.

In spite of the many ways in which the expression 'planning' has been used, there are some important general ideas which link the different meanings and provide a focus for an account of the politics of economic planning. In popular usage, a plan involves an objective and a set of actions designed to achieve that objective. An individual's plans may include economic actions – about production or consumption, for example – but when we talk of 'economic planning' we are really talking about the planning of economic activity by some central authority. The key idea is that the state is to undertake the role of setting economic objectives and selecting suitable actions in order to attain these objectives. At any stage, those who call for more economic planning are those who believe that, in certain areas at least, the role of the government in economic activity should be increased. They will differ, however, on the precise form of the objectives and on the actions required.

It would be almost impossible to find anyone in this country who believes that the government should do no planning at all, but there is a spectrum along which the disputants can be ranged. (It is an over-simplification to treat the spectrum as uni-dimensional. The triumph of Keynesian 'planning' was a defeat for a different form of planning which involved considerable intervention in individual industries.) The idea of a spectrum helps to explain why the precise meaning of planning has shifted through time. Before the Second World War the idea that the government had the duty and the ability to control the level of unemployment was novel if not revolutionary. The attempts to exert such control were described then as planning. It was in this sense that Oliver Stanley in 1934 remarked, 'We are all planners now.' After the war it was generally accepted that the government was responsible for controlling the overall level of economic activity; by the late 1950s the 'planners' were those who argued that the government should increase the rate of growth of output. Further along the spectrum were those who argued that the government should accept responsibility for planning not only the level of activity but also its composition – so much steel, so many cars, etc.

Finally, at the present time, economic planning tends to imply the setting of long- or medium-term objectives (of five years or more) – in contrast to the kind of short-term management of the economy which has typified economic policy in most of the post-war period.

In his important book, *The Principles of Economic Planning* (1948), W. A. Lewis defined economic planning as 'Government action designed to secure results different from those of the market.' That would now seem far too broad a definition. It would cover every possible type of regulation, from safety regulations and licensing hours to full-scale control of consumption and industrial output. Also it seems too negative; the government must have some positive objective other than simply to interfere with the market. However the definition does emphasize an extremely important point which will be developed in the next chapter. If individuals do not plan their activities the result tends to be at best disorder and at worst death from starvation. However it does not necessarily follow that a country's economic decisions – about what is to be produced and how and who is to consume it – need overall or central planning. Certainly the government ought to plan its own economic activities, but that does not mean that it ought to plan everybody else's. An important tradition of economic thought argues that, on the contrary, economic decisions are best left to the individual and that the onus of proving that interference helps must lie on those who wish to interfere. The market is the mechanism by which individual plans are coordinated in the absence of government intervention; thus the market stands as the rival institution to the call for more economic planning. And those who defend the market argue that if the government wants to intervene, if it wants to impose its own objectives on the economy, it should as far as possible do so by using market forces.

THE POLITICS OF PLANNING

A study of the politics of planning should be distinguished from either a history of or a textbook on planning, though it will most closely resemble the former. We are concerned to identify the parties and interest groups involved, to explain their attitudes to planning and to trace how their conflicts are resolved through the political process. By contrast with the politics of medicine, for example, the relevant interest groups are not easily identifiable. This is because economic planning is likely to be only a part, and not a major part, of any single group's objectives. Further, economic planning is a technique. There is no *a priori* reason to associate it with a particular party or a particular class.

Nevertheless, although as a technique it may be neutral, we find in practice that in Britain planning receives more support from the left than from the right. What is more, economic planning tends to be particularly associated with the Labour Party As Joan Mitchell says, 'Economic planning was originally, and still is largely, a policy advocated by Socialists.'[6] Thus much of the politics of economic planning is party politics, and we approach its history mainly in terms of the ideas and actions of the two major parties. The Labour Party is associated with planning for two main reasons. The first is the belief held by Labour supporters that the interests of those whom the party represents are best met by planning The second is that since the war the Labour Party has wanted planning to be its distinctive approach to economic policy. It needs such a distinctive approach both as a sales device and for internal cohesion. The post-war history of economic planning in the Labour Party can be seen as its attempt to find a creed to replace its pre-war commitment to public ownership.

Economic planning, as I have said, is largely identified with the left. We have not had the extreme forms of right-wing planned capitalism as experienced before the war in Italy, Germany and Japan. But there is a cycle of general opinion, of all parties and groups, which moves for and against planning. These moves can occasionally, as they did in 1961, leave the left stranded, with the Conservatives appearing as the proponents of planning. We need to understand why these moves occur. Do the initiatives come from the political parties, and if so, to what pressures are they responding? Or do they come from outside, for example from the trade unions or the employers' groups or from economic events outside political control? I shall suggest that the forces are often non-political in the sense that they reflect both external events and the development of the economic debate. If that is true, the parties adopt or abandon planning in the way that maintains their support and best preserves their proclaimed political beliefs.

The two parties are the major participants in the planning debate, but at particular points in this account I shall also examine the influence of the trade union movement and of the CBI and its precursors. Less easy to define but no less important is the middle-class tradition of benevolent social concern which unites Tories and Fabians. It is a tradition which prevails in legislation and administration.

What interests are at stake in the extension of economic planning? The most straightforward issues are those of material reward. Who will gain economically and who will lose? And there is also the question of the distribution of power. Economic power, under the market system, is allocated according to income and wealth. Marxists argue that economic power resides disproportionately with the owners of capital. Calls for planning are partly a call for the redistribution of economic power: to take power away from the rich or the capitalists and to entrust decisions about the allocation of resources to the people, as represented by parliament. Calls for planning are thus frequently associated with calls for public ownership. At other times calls for planning involve a less fundamental shift in economic power. Currently, the left wing of the Labour Party would like power to be taken away from the multi-national corporations; at other times it has wanted to take power away from the Treasury. These shifts in power are one of the aspects of planning that give rise to political conflict.

ECONOMISTS AND PLANNING

Economists can be thought of as an interest group rather than as a pressure group. Their views are by no means free of personal or political bias; but they do not speak with one voice and are to be found on both sides of the planning debate. Their most important contribution should be to define the limits of what planning and markets can achieve within the constraints of a mixed economy open to foreign trade. Some economists have gone beyond these tasks to contribute to the more general political debate about whether there is any room for planning in a liberal democracy.

As in all intellectual history, it is extremely difficult to determine the impact of economic knowledge on decisions. Economists are rarely so united as to offer unequivocal advice, and politicians generally refer neither to economists nor to economic theories when announcing decisions, so we can only dimly detect the implied theory and its author. We are concerned here with economics as only one influence among many in the process of political decision. Usually politicians receive a wide range of advice, and the interesting question is why one view is adopted rather than another.

There is a much-quoted passage at the end of Keynes's *General Theory* which says, '. . . the ideas of economists and political philosophers, both when they are right and when they are wrong, are more powerful than is commonly understood. Indeed, the world is ruled by little else. Practical men, who believe themselves to be quite exempt from any intellectual influences, are usually the slaves of some defunct economist.'

Keynes appeared to have in mind two traditions: the laissez-faire policies of the liberal economists and the utilitarianism of the political philosophers. The two were linked to justify minimal intervention in economic and social matters and to defend the wealth and power of the successful capitalist. The influence of economists has certainly waned since Keynes's claim. Samuel Brittan has shown[7] that there is now far greater agreement on policy issues among economists of all political persuasions than between economists and non-economists (including politicians). This is less true of macro-economic issues (those which concern the overall management of the economy) than of micro-economic issues (concerned, for example, with such issues as the pricing of railway journeys). This is not because politicians have fallen behind the advances of economics – since most of the micro-economic questions that Brittan asked would have been answered identically by economists fifty or even a hundred years ago. It is the politicians themselves who have changed and the most important cause of this change is Keynes himself.

THE TECHNIQUES OF PLANNING

This book is concerned with decisions about planning and with the general political debate about it, rather than with planning techniques, but a brief account is presented here to help the reader understand some of the practical ideas involved. The question of techniques does in practice impinge on the political debate, since attempts at planning raise the important question of the political control of the planners themselves, for planning could simply involve the transfer of economic power from one minority group – the capitalists, for example – to the bureaucrats. This danger has always been stressed by the opponents of planning – though they tend to talk in terms of the transfer of economic power from the people to the bureaucrats – and it has been raised by some writers on the left, notably Richard Crossman.[8]

Related to this is the question of how far parliament is a suitable arena for the discussion of economic policy. It was raised forcefully by Churchill in his Romanes lectures of 1930. He argued that parliament was an excellent institution for resolving straightforward questions of interest; but economic policy would often involve imposing unpopular measures on all major parties. There is always the risk that one party will claim that the unpopular measures are unnecessary and thereby seek an electoral advantage.

Churchill's solution was to establish an Economic Parliament, 'free altogether from party exigencies, and composed of persons possessing special qualifications in such matters.'[9] The view that the discussion of economic policy should be removed from parliament was commonly expressed on both the left and the right before the war. Its modern equivalent is the suggestion that Britain's economic policy should be run by successful big businessmen; and it was also reflected in Edward Heath's determination to seek administrative solutions to Britain's problems, particularly inflation.

The problems of administration are most severe when governments are trying to undertake detailed economic planning. There are two problems: first, how are objectives to be set; second, how are they to be attained. All planning is an exercise in what is known, in the jargon of operations research, as maximization subject to constraints. The constraints include the technical properties of the economy in terms of its resources and productive techniques. They also include the behaviour of those parts of the economy which cannot be controlled directly, though they can be influenced indirectly. For example if an important part of a plan is a target for exports, the government, while it cannot force other countries to buy our exports, may encourage them to do so by making exports cheaper through subsidies. This 'maximization' applies to all the government's social and economic objectives. It will have a rough idea of the 'trade-offs' involved in any policy decision, so much extra employment, for example, will be worth so much extra inflation.

During the war the major objectives were clearly defined and the government exercised considerable direct control over the economy via rationing, construction licensing, and its control of raw materials. Planning could therefore be conducted in physical terms; that is, immediate objectives could be set in terms of so many aircraft, so many tanks and so on, and the objectives could be attained by allocating raw materials and labour to specific factories. Choices had to be made between different types of military equipment and between civilian and military needs for resources.

These were political and strategic decisions. Providing information about what was feasible and deciding which factory should produce what was the responsibility of the planning officials.

After the war, such methods were soon abandoned. Planning then became a question of setting targets for output for the major industries. The targets were a mixture of the feasible and the desirable. The government, aided by its officials, decided how much coal and cotton it wanted subject to available resources. The exercise was conducted in terms of 'budgets' of manpower and physical resources. Import controls and some rationing of consumer goods provided a measure of direct control of the economy, but in general, the government had very little power to ensure that its desires were met; the results were correspondingly disappointing.

When that experiment was abandoned, 'planning' was transformed into managing the level of demand along Keynesian lines. Objectives were set – for the level of output, the rate of inflation and the balance of payments. The procedure was then for officials to make a forecast of what would happen to the economy, over a period of about a year, if policies were unchanged. If the foreseen outcome was unsatisfactory in some way, taxes or government expenditure would be changed to bring the economy closer to the desired state. If unemployment was too high, taxes would be cut and/or government expenditure would be increased. If the balance of payments deficit were too large, the opposite policy changes would be made. If both unemployment was too high and the balance of payments deficit was too large, the government had to decide which of the two objectives took priority.

This style of economic management held sway throughout the 1950s. It emphasized demand management and assumed that, within limits, supply would adjust to whatever level of demand was generated by the government's policies. Thus, in the short run, the government could make output grow faster or slower as it wished. In 1962 demand management was supplemented by an attempt to plan the supply side of the economy. This was something of a return to the planning exercises of the immediate post-war period but the theory and techniques were rather different. The government set medium-term objectives for the growth of output and its components – public expenditure, investment, private consumption, exports and imports. It also investigated the industrial implications of attaining the targets. The objectives were almost certainly unattainable, but that is another story. The planning technique used was 'input-output analysis'. This technique recognizes the flows of commodities between industries: the production of a ton of coal for final consumption requires so much steel, so much electricity, so much labour, etc. The production of a ton of steel requires so much coal, so much electricity, so much labour, etc. Input-output analysis shows how much of each commodity and how much labour is needed to meet a particular pattern of final demand. The technique was used more fully (though still very sketchily) by the Labour Government in 1964 and 1965. The theory was that the results of input-output analysis would tell all industries what they would have to produce if the government's overall objectives were to be met. Further, if the industries had faith in the government's capacity to achieve these objectives, they could be confident that their own output would find a market. This was known as 'indicative planning'; the government did not offer any direct measures to ensure that the output was forthcoming, but it used demand management to try to get the process started.

After the abandonment of the National Plan in 1966, there were no further attempts at that kind of exercise. The most recent form of planning, introduced by the Labour Government, is described as Industrial Strategy. Inasmuch as it means anything, it means encouraging individual companies to expand investment and employment, possibly by the use of planning agreements. In a planning agreement the government is supposed to make certain promises about sales and possibly about financial assistance, while the company makes certain promises about employment and industrial relations. How this is supposed to fit in with some overall view of the development of the economy is not yet known.

PLANNING AND PRICES

This study deals only peripherally with attempts to control inflation by direct intervention in wages and prices. This is partly because such policies are not usually thought of or described as economic planning. There are periods when the control of inflation by direct measures such as wage and price policies becomes the central issue of economic policy, possibly in conjunction with economic planning in the familiar sense. Any attempts to direct the structure of output must involve some solution to the problem of how labour and material resources are to be allocated, which inevitably will raise issues of pay and price policy.

Economists distinguish between questions of *relative* prices and wages (e.g. the price of butter relative to the price of margarine) and the *absolute level* of prices and wages (i.e. the movement in all prices). During most of the post-war period the emphasis has been on the latter; more particularly it has been on the rate of inflation, the rate of increase in the absolute level of prices. If we talk of planning in this context we can say that governments have tried to plan the absolute level of prices rather than the structure of relative prices.

Attempts to control the rate of inflation by wages and prices policies involve particular views of how the economy works. In general, those who propose such policies tend to believe that wages are not determined within the economic system itself; they emphasize instead such explanations as trade union militancy or loss of social discipline. The role of incomes policies in their view is to offset these undesirable social tendencies. They may however have a residual belief that economic forces do have some influence on the rate of wage increase.

The nature of these residual beliefs can change quite sharply. For most of the post-war period it was generally believed that the level of unemployment had some effect on the rate of wage increase. Thus attempts to make the economy grow more rapidly by expanding demand (and thus increasing employment levels) might cause a short-run acceleration of inflation. Planning linked to incomes policies attempted to suppress this inflation. But after the 1960s the link between high levels of employment and wage inflation seemed to have been broken. Wages and unemployment soared together. A new explanation was put forward: aspiration for 'real' wage increases was responsible for inflation. The belief was that unions decided how much real wages should grow and set their claims accordingly. If they failed to get their target increase one year they would demand even more the following year. If that theory is true, one way of reducing wage inflation is to make the economy grow faster – increasing real earnings. In this way, economic planning would be able to increase economic growth and control wage inflation simultaneously.

The planning of wages and prices is thus important to this study in two ways. Attempts to alter the structure of the economy involve controlling *relative* wages and prices. The government can either intervene in prices and wages or can allocate resources (including labour) by direct order. The insistence of the trade union movement on free collective bargaining and their rejection of labour direction can rule out both and thus render this kind of planning impossible. This has been suggested as an explanation for the abandonment of planning during 1945–51. In recent years there has been more emphasis on *absolute* prices, on the rate of inflation. In this context, planning to achieve more rapid economic growth may be seen as one way of controlling inflation. Alternatively, the policy-makers may believe that although rapid growth helps to control inflation in the long run, it may make it worse in the short run. In such cases an incomes policy may be introduced at the same time as an economic plan. The impact of incomes policies on relative wages is treated as a minor problem.

I believe that the normal justification for the use of incomes policies to control inflation is wrong. The post-war approach to the control of inflation is based not only on a misunderstanding of the way in which absolute prices are determined, but also on a neglect of the importance of relative prices. As a result, incomes policies have no long-run effect on inflation but, since they reduce the adjustment of relative wages and prices, have harmful effects on the whole structure of the British economy. Ultimately, they add to our economic problems rather than solve them.

Chapter 2: The Background to the Debate

The planning debate of the 1930s differed from that of the 1960s both in the kind of problems that planning was intended to solve and in the proposed techniques, and, above all, in the general view about how the economy worked. All this makes it hard to define a single set of key issues that determined attitudes to planning. My main concern at this stage is to describe the current state of the debate and to provide a general guide to the changing ideas that fired it in the past. The historical perspective reminds us how little we seem to have learnt and how much we have forgotten. This is strikingly illustrated in some of the present discussions on economic policy, which mirror similar debates of forty years ago and cast doubt on much that has been believed for at least twenty-five years.

Our discussion is concerned both with the economic arguments for and against intervention and planning, and with economic policy in the wider sense. When James Callaghan announces that it is not possible for a country to 'spend its way out of unemployment', he is denying what has been the basis of economic policy for the last twenty-five years. Whether or not he is right, such statements have very important implications for the future of the debate on planning. If the government is expressing doubts about conventional economic policy, the claims that it should be replaced by planning are likely to grow stronger.

The question of how much economic planning there should be and what form it should take is part of the wider question of what role the state ought to play in running the economy. Can the economy be left to run itself, or does the state have a duty to direct some or all of it? Supporters of planning believe that the government should set targets for the performance of the economy, and should introduce the policy measures needed to achieve them. In the extreme case the government would decide what should be produced, how it should be produced and who should get it. No one is seriously proposing that extreme version of the command economy, and there is considerable debate, even among economists and planners, about what the scope of economic planning should be and what techniques should be used. But there still remains a general question about the need for government intervention and direction.

The current convention is to distinguish between the micro-economic and macro-economic aspects of the question. The former refers to the activities of individual consumers and producers or to the behaviour of particular markets, and the latter refers to total economic behaviour – the level of output, the level of unemployment, etc. I shall adopt the convention, but with some very important *caveats*. The first is that the distinction is a post-war one and it is misleading to squeeze the pre-war debate into it. The second is that the boundaries between the two may be unclear. The planning of investment, for example, may be a question of micro-economics or of macro-economics. The third and most important is that the distinction begs some fundamental questions in economics.

Economics textbooks at the undergraduate level and beyond either deal quite separately with macro- and micro-economics or deal with only one or the other. Economists tend to do the same. This division arises not only from a belief in the benefits of the division of labour but also from the near-impossibility of believing in micro- and macro-economics simultaneously. In a nutshell, micro-economics emphasizes the role of markets whereas macro-economics ignores them completely. Where have the markets gone to in macro-economics? Keynesian economics, in a simplified form, had such an enormous effect on economics and economic policy that it is only fairly recently that the question has been raised; for most of the post-war era the problem did not worry anybody.

It is helpful to distinguish three broad positions in the planning debate. The supporters of the first share a general belief in markets. Within the group there are different views on the extent to which markets need correction, on the desirable scope of public expenditure and, most importantly, on the need to redistribute income and wealth. Sam Brittan describes this group as believers in 'corrected markets'.[1] Members of this group tend to describe themselves as liberals, though ironically this term has been captured in the United States by those who believe in intervention. Although the liberals disagree among themselves about how much correction capitalism needs, they all accept a common framework for resolving the issues.

The second group is more readily defined by what it does not believe in than by what it does. It is wrong to think of it as standing between the other two groups, since it includes a wide range of political opinion; but its characteristic member is a political moderate who rejects both socialism and liberalism in their extreme forms. The group can loosely be described as 'Keynesian' in the sense that its members emphasize the government's responsibility for the overall management of the economy in terms of unemployment, inflation and the balance of payments. They are sceptical about the role of markets both in relation to microeconomic questions and in relation to the behaviour of the economy as a whole. They are also somewhat sceptical about economic planning but do not oppose it strongly. This group dominates informed opinion in Britain and includes most politicians and civil servants. Recent economic history has cast serious doubts on their position.

The third group in the debate, which stands generally on the far left, rejects the framework completely. At the extreme, they argue that no system which contains capitalism is defensible and that there is therefore no useful purpose in discussing how it could be corrected. Along with the rejection of capitalism tends to go a rejection of markets, or at least doubts about their usefulness.

THE LIBERAL TRADITION

The first group discusses the problems of economic policy within a set of ideas variously described as 'liberal', 'individualist', 'neo-classical' or 'bourgeois'. I shall use the expression 'neo-classical'. The tradition derives from the writings of the eighteenth-century liberals, particularly Adam Smith; they were developed by Ricardo and refined by Marshall and others towards the end of the nineteenth century.

Neo-classical economics stresses the behaviour of the individual, who is pictured choosing his occupation and spending his income in the way which, subject to the constraints of his endowments of wealth and abilities, produces the greatest satisfaction. It can be shown that, under certain conditions, such individual behaviour by consumers and producers operating in perfectly competitive markets produces an outcome which is 'optimal' in the sense that no one can be made better off without making someone else worse off. (This is known as Pareto optimality.) An optimal outcome is achieved because, under perfect competition, if individuals were not arranging their purposes so as to maximize their satisfaction, it would pay them to rearrange them, and if goods were not being produced in the most efficient way, it would pay someone to enter the industry and produce them more efficiently.

The implication of the argument is that organizing production and consumption efficiently can be left to individual decisions and freely operating markets. There is no need for any overall guidance or planning of the national economy. In the neo-classical tradition, the case for planning is a negative one; it can only be justified to the extent that markets operating on their own are not achieving a Pareto optimum.

We shall consider some of the conditions that are necessary for this result in due course; but some comments about the Pareto optimum can be made now. The expression 'Pareto optimum' has probably never been used in public debate, and this is hardly surprising since it is not only an extremely complicated idea but it is also extremely politically uninteresting. The great political issues are usually precisely those in which someone *is* made worse off in order to make someone else better off. Also a Pareto optimal position is not necessarily the best one to choose; we may prefer situations which are not Pareto optimal but which have a preferred distribution of income. Nevertheless, economists find it useful to discuss Pareto optima because they reduce the need to make value-judgments. Also they argue that it is worth moving to a Pareto optimum if such a move can be combined with an income distribution which is politically desirable.

Even under these conditions there are cases where market forces clearly do not produce an efficient allocation of resources. These have always been accepted by neo-classical economists as grounds for interference in the market. We list them briefly since they call for intervention rather than planning in its popular sense. The first problem is that monopolies may develop for technical and legal reasons. If monopolists are allowed to pursue their own interests freely, the result will be socially inefficient. A second problem are the goods and services which cannot be provided through markets. The classic examples are defence and police services. These 'public goods' provide benefits to the general public and it is not possible to devise a pricing system to charge users according to the amount of the good they use. A third limitation is that the efficiency of the market system is based on response to prices. For the efficient allocation of resources, the price of a good or service must be equal to the total cost to society of producing it. In some cases, the private cost diverges from the social cost. A smoking factory chimney is a familiar example. The cost and inconvenience is borne by nearby households and not by the factory, and the price paid for the goods produced by the factory therefore does not reflect the full social cost of producing them. Another familiar example is the cost of motoring to the private individual, which does not include the costs of pollution and congestion that he imposes on society.

These problems – monopoly, public goods, and the divergence between social costs and benefits and private costs and benefits – have long been recognized by the neo-classical tradition. The support for laissez-faire has been tempered by them, and their solution calls for state powers which in turn involve a variety of interventions ranging from taxes and subsidies to statutory controls. Their use generally involves politics and the interests of those whose activities are being regulated. In other words, a move towards efficiency is usually accompanied by a redistribution of income or wealth, and it is the latter which causes the political problems.

These problems raise the case for intervention and the extension of state power, but do not in themselves justify economic planning. The government need not in the liberal scheme of things decide how to organize the economy by setting objectives or directives, except in the small area of direct activity – the maintenance of a legal framework, for example – that these causes justify.

Present-day extreme liberal economists, F. A. Hayek and Milton Friedman for example, stop here.[2] Apart from control of the money supply and any necessary action to redistribute income and wealth, they would resist further extension of the state's economic role. By their standards, there is already too much intervention and planning in the British economy. At certain points they admit the inadequacy of markets, for example in providing for children (who cannot make sensible economic decisions), but do not necessarily accept the current alternative solutions. Other liberal economists are far more prepared to believe either that markets are not efficiently meeting individuals' preferences or accept that individuals' preferences should sometimes be overruled. However they will only interfere reluctantly, and even when they do interfere they will prefer to do so through the use of markets.

Of the special conditions required to prove the efficiency of perfectly competitive markets, the most important is the assumption that there is perfect certainty about the future. It is this point which separates the men from the boys as far as liberal economics is concerned. The extreme liberals accept that there is uncertainty but argue that it does not provide a case for intervention or planning. The moderate liberals, while accepting the general case for the use of markets, believe that uncertainty does cause problems which require government attention. This is particularly so in the case of investment (expenditure on capital goods) which essentially involves guesswork about future demand. In addition they believe that even if markets work, some markets, notably the market for labour, adjust so slowly that it is up to the government to speed the process along, otherwise there may be an unacceptable level of unemployment. They thus believe, to use the current terms, that competition and markets work efficiently at the micro-economic level but do not work efficiently at the macro-economic level. In questions of macro-economics they therefore find themselves closer to the group sceptical of both markets and socialism.

KEYNES AND DEMAND MANAGEMENT

This group has been heavily influenced by the work of Keynes. The importance of Keynes in the debate on government intervention and in forming attitudes to planning cannot be overstated. He provided what most people believe is the main case for the state's role in managing the overall behaviour of the economy. At the same time he destroyed the Labour Party's pre-war case for detailed planning.

Rather than provide a detailed history of the development of Keynes's ideas (there is a valuable brief account in D. E. Moggridge, *Keynes*[3]) it is more appropriate in this context to describe the main elements of his work as they were absorbed into the mainstream of economic thought. Keynes was seeking to explain – and remedy – the appallingly high levels of unemployment of the 1930s. He set himself to challenge the neo-classical theories then current, which asserted that unemployment must either be voluntary or a temporary phenomenon which would disappear as markets adjusted.

Since both explanations seemed to be patently untrue, theories based on the assumption that markets worked perfectly were unacceptable. The policy reaction was, as far as the Conservative and National Governments were concerned, to interfere with markets and to organize cartels and limit competition. The socialist opposition, which needed far less persuasion that market capitalism was inefficient, was calling for public ownership and planning. Keynes offered an alternative to the neo-classical theory but his policy conclusions were very different from those of the socialists.

3

Keynes's theory came to be accepted almost completely. During the course of its wide acceptance it was simplified and modified until much of its original flavour and the particular circumstances which saw its birth were forgotten. It is only recently, when the simplified version of Keynesian economics has seemed to fail, that there has been extensive reconsideration of Keynes's full arguments and of his other writings on economics. In the simple version of Keynes's theory, emphasis is shifted away from supply and demand in individual markets to supply and demand in the economy as a whole. To present the matter very briefly, supply is represented by the incomes people receive (since they are paid for producing output) and demand is represented by their desired expenditure out of their incomes. The desired expenditure of households and firms will thus determine output. What people do not spend on consumer goods – their savings – has to equal that part of output not devoted to consumer goods, namely, investment. The economy has to adjust until the two are equal to each other.

Keynes stressed this equilibrium condition, as he had in his earlier *Treatise on Money*, because decisions on investment and decisions on savings were carried out by different people and there was therefore (he argued) no direct way of coordinating the two sets of decisions; changes in output had to bear the brunt of the adjustment. Keynes argued that the 'equilibrium' level at which total supply was equal to total demand would not necessarily be one of full employment. Full employment was simply a special case of his 'general' theory. It was therefore up to the government, in the conditions of the 1930s, to expand demand by one means or another in order to expand output and hence reduce unemployment.

We shall consider, in due course, the implications of this view for post-war economic policy, and the recent attacks on the theory, but it is worth examining what Keynes thought the implications were for socialism and planning. Keynes had set out his ideas on socialism earlier in his essay 'The End of Laissez-Faire'. He dismissed state socialism as 'little better than a dusty survival of a plan to meet the problem of fifty years ago, based on a misunderstanding of what someone said a hundred years ago.'[4] He defined the limits of government intervention as follows: 'The important thing for Government is not to do things which individuals are doing already, and to do them a little better or a little worse; but to do those things which at present are not done at all.'[5]

Keynes did not provide a full list of such possible activities, but he named some. He said that many of the greatest economic evils of the time arose from risk, uncertainty and ignorance. They included unemployment, for which his solutions were the central control of currency and of credit and public dissemination of business data. His second example was savings and investment:

I believe that some coordinated act of intelligent judgement is required as to the scale on which it is desirable that the community as a whole should save, the scale on which these savings should go abroad in the form of foreign investments, and whether the present organization of the investment market distributes savings along the most nationally productive channels.[6]

He did not think that such matters should be left to private judgement and private profits. He thus agreed with the socialists that investment was too important a matter to be left to markets. But unlike them, he thought that the solution was to improve the techniques of capitalism. He argued that capitalism, wisely managed, could probably be made more efficient for attaining economic ends than any alternative system yet in sight; but he believed that it was also in many ways extremely objectionable and that alternatives – other than socialism – should be sought.

What policy conclusions did Keynes draw specifically from *The General Theory*? As so often, he became strongly involved in the policy debate. In January 1937 he published a series of articles in *The Times* entitled 'How to Avoid a Slump'. By that time, the post-1932 cheap money policy, together with a managed exchange rate, had produced a boom, which started in housing and spread to other types of investment. Keynes was concerned to avoid future fluctuations in demand. He argued that the boom should be controlled to avoid a possible collapse of investment if expectations were disappointed, and he suggested that a programme of short-lived public investment projects should be kept in stock. He also argued that the long-term interest rate should be kept close to its long-term optimum, and that it should not be used as a weapon of short-term demand management. He believed that deficient demand would be the main long-term problem and proposed the use of tax policy, tariff reductions and public works to extend the boom. These proposals had some effect immediately, but their full force was not felt till after the war.

In the final pages of *The General Theory*, Keynes turned to its implications for 'social philosophy'. In many ways, his comments are strongly anti-capitalist. He wanted to reduce interest rates sharply so that savings were equal to investment when there was full employment. This would leave the owner of capital with just enough return to cover costs of production '*plus* an allowance for risk and the skills of supervision'. He continued: 'Now, though this state of affairs would be quite compatible with some measure of individualism, yet it would mean the euthanasia of the rentier, and, consequently, the euthanasia of the cumulative oppressive power of the capitalist to exploit the scarcity value of capital.'[7]

On the question of the role of the state, Keynes described his theory as 'moderately conservative in its implications'. The state should regulate consumption by monetary and fiscal measures. It would also probably (since interest rates would not be an adequate instrument) have to take some direct responsibility for the level of investment, 'though this need not exclude all manner of compromises and of devices, by which public authority will cooperate with private initiative'.[8] Beyond that, he made out no case for state socialism. If central controls succeeded in establishing full employment, the classical theory would come into its own again:

If we suppose the volume of output to be given, i.e. to be determined by forces outside the classical scheme of thought, then there is no objection to be raised against the classical analysis of the manner in which private self-interest will determine what in particular is produced, in what proportions the factors of production will be combined to produce it, and how the value of the final product will be distributed between them.[9]

Although the achievement of full employment would involve a large extension of the functions of government, Keynes was determined to leave a wide field in which 'the traditional advantages of individualism would still hold good'. He regarded individualism as the best safeguard of personal liberty. 'It is also the best safeguard of the variety of life, which emerges precisely from this extended field of personal choice, and the loss of which is the greatest of all the losses of the homogeneous or totalitarian state.'[10]

The full impact of Keynes's ideas was not felt until the end of the war. The pre-war Treasury was hostile to his views. The budget of 1941 was based on his approach to the potential inflationary problem of the war, but this was something of a false dawn, and the problem was one of excess demand rather than unemployment. The first open acceptance of the government's responsibility for controlling unemployment was in the Coalition Government's White Paper on Employment Policy,[11] although it only included a modest statement of Keynes's approach.

In terms of planning, the most important immediate effect was on the Labour Party. Insofar as it was basing its case for public ownership and planning on the need to control unemployment, Keynes was threatening to pull the rug from beneath it. Yet the idea that the government should try to manage the general level of economic activity was revolutionary enough for the Labour Party to dub Keynesian demand management 'planning'. For even though it fell far short of the Labour Party's proposals, it marked a considerable extension of the government's responsibilities. Moreover, demand management seemed successful enough after the war, and the Labour case for more detailed planning was lost.

KEYNESIANISM IN ECLIPSE?

In a speech to the Labour Party Conference in September 1976 James Callaghan said:

> We used to think that you could just spend your way out of a recession and increase employment by cutting taxes and boosting government spending. I tell you in all candour that that option no longer exists, and that insofar as it ever did exist, it worked by injecting inflation into the economy. And each time that happened the average level of unemployment has risen. Higher inflation, followed by higher unemployment. That is the history of the last twenty years.

This is an extraordinarily important admission, even if its immediate intention was political. It reflects the doubts that are now felt about Keynesian economic policy. These doubts, which were already being expressed in academic circles, came to the fore during and after the Conservative policies of 1970 to 1974. The doubts apply less to Keynes's ideas than to the uses to which they have been put.

The General Theory was written as an exercise in polemics to correct what Keynes thought was a mistaken approach to the problem of unemployment. The ideas incorporated in it continued to be used after the war during conditions of generally low unemployment. As time went on (the details are discussed in Chapter 5) the policies seemed to run ever more rapidly into problems of the balance of payments or of inflation. By the time of the economic plans of the 1960s it was believed that the problem of inflation could be solved by the use of incomes policies. As far as the balance of payments was concerned, the government apparently thought that growth itself and the incomes policy would solve the problem. Others believed that a flexible exchange rate was the answer.

These experiences did not destroy the basic confidence in Keynesian ideas. There were few who doubted that the government could at least control the level of unemployment. The planning experiment of the 1960s was intended to supplement conventional demand management, not to replace it. But the new doubts about Keynesian economics and rival theories now proposed suggested that much of the history of post-war economic policy should be re-written. In particular, it is argued that the weakness of sterling, so often given as the explanation for the failure of the planning experiment, was a symptom not a cause of the problem. The earlier adoption of devaluation or flexible exchange rates would not have made much difference.

The policies of 1970 to 1974 produced a combination of high unemployment, near-disastrous inflation and a record balance of payments deficit, in spite of the fact that the government abandoned the fixed exchange rate and introduced a series of incomes policies. In the general confusion at these failures, the most serious intellectual challenge came from those economists who emphasized the importance of money in the economy. It was this group who were popularly believed to have been completely routed by the triumph of Keynesianism. The recent revival of 'monetarism' has been linked with the views of the extreme liberal economists, who assert that the government should not accept any responsibility for the overall level of economic activity.

It is difficult to do justice to the monetarists' analysis in a brief account, but a general outline can be given. They argue that, left to itself, the economy will tend to settle at a level of unemployment, the 'natural' rate of unemployment, at which all markets, including the market for labour, are in balance. Any attempt by the government to reduce unemployment below its natural rate will lead to accelerating inflation, balance of payments difficulties or both. The nature of the inflationary process in the economy will depend on whether exchange rates are fixed or flexible. If they are fixed, Britain's rate of inflation will be determined principally by the rate of inflation in the rest of the world. If the money supply grows too rapidly, the result will be a deterioration in the balance of payments. If exchange rates are flexible, Britain's rate of inflation will, in the long run, depend on the rate of growth of the money supply. Rapid growth of the money supply will be accompanied by a rapid decline in the exchange rate.

If the monetarists are correct, the government cannot have any permanent influence on the level of economic activity, and thus on unemployment; it can only influence the rate of inflation – and it can only do that if exchange rates are flexible. The problems of the late 1950s and 1960s arose, according to monetarist theory, because governments were trying to keep unemployment at too low a level. They were deceived by the successes of the early 1950s but those were due largely to an excessive devaluation of the pound in 1949 and to favourable movements in raw material prices. Since the exchange rate was fixed after 1949, Britain's rate of inflation could not depart seriously from that of the rest of the world, and any policies which might have led to over-expansion of the money-supply had to be reversed when their impact was felt on the balance of payments. A flexible exchange rate would not have helped matters; attempts to keep unemployment below its natural rate would simply have resulted in inflation rather than balance of payments crises. Incomes policies could only have provided a temporary solution. Since the diagnosis of the problem was wrong, the National Plan of 1965 was bound to fail, just as the later devaluation and abandonment of the fixed exchange rate did.

The monetarist arguments appear to challenge the whole of Keynes's ideas. In fact they are consistent with much that he wrote, particularly in his earlier book, *The Treatise on Money*; but there are some important issues which separate the monetarists and extreme liberals from more moderate liberals and the middle-of-the-road Keynesians. The two which are most relevant to a discussion of economic planning are the questions of investment and unemployment. At this point we take up the account of neo-classical economics where we left it, in the discussion of uncertainty.

UNCERTAINTY, INVESTMENT AND
UNEMPLOYMENT

The liberals argue that the coordination of economic activity should be left to the market. If it is, there will undoubtedly be occasional mistakes, which may be major. Goods will be produced which nobody wants. People with painfully acquired skills may suddenly find that these skills are no longer required. Entire industries may lose markets. The defenders of planning believe that planning can avoid such mistakes, or can at least reduce the problems associated with uncertainty.

It is obvious that since the future is unknown, we inevitably make mistakes, in economic life as elsewhere. The question is, how well can the market cope with it and can planning by a central authority do better? Society, particularly capitalist society, has devised a number of institutions to deal with the problem of uncertainty. Insurance is an obvious example, but there are also forward markets, futures markets and stock markets, which trade in claims on the uncertain revenues from companies. The desirable property of such markets is not that they should remove uncertainty completely – that is impossible – but that we should know what will happen under all possible contingencies and be able to protect ourselves as far as the market will allow. For example I cannot tell whether or not my house will burn down next year, but at least I know that I shall be compensated if it does burn down. The technical problem is that for markets to be efficient in conditions of uncertainty we need *complete* markets, which must cover all possible future contingencies. That is quite impossible, so the question is whether the government should intervene on our behalf and plan for our security.

The extreme liberals believe that the incompleteness of markets is not serious and certainly does not justify planning, but the moderate liberals are more cautious. They believe that there may be some case for planning investment, since it most importantly involves decisions about the future. However their proposals (for indicative planning, for example) are more concerned with the exchange of information than with government direction.

The remaining problem, which presents the most serious difficulty, is that of unemployment. Even if it is accepted that there is a natural rate of unemployment, the economy may get stuck at a higher level and be unable to adjust. It is quite clear that the labour market cannot adjust rapidly to changed conditions; there are high costs to changing jobs and even higher costs to moving from one part of Britain to another. The idea that unemployed workers can find jobs by offering to work at below the current wage is quite unrealistic. If wages are generally too high, it will be a long time before workers realize this, and a long time before the required adjustment in real wages will take place. The extreme liberals think that the adjustment can take place quite rapidly, particularly if obstacles to mobility, such as the prohibition on exchanging council houses and the discouragement of private letting, are removed. They also argue that intervention by governments delays the eventual adjustment and leaves us with an increasingly unsuitable and archaic economic structure.

Unemployment presents a hard case. Those who argue that there are no grounds for intervention must be satisfied that the appalling unemployment levels of the 1930s were due to a succession of policy mistakes (by foreign as well as by British governments). In general, liberal economists do not deny that there are serious problems in relying on markets, and will accept that investment and unemployment are two of them, but in the end they do not rely solely on their economic beliefs. They have a general doubt whether central planning could do better and, given this doubt, they believe the market is to be preferred for its political virtues. Reliance on the market not only encourages the qualities of independence and enterprise, it also prevents coercion by the state. In Milton Friedman's words:

Historical evidence speaks with a single voice on the relation between political freedom and a free market. I know of no example in time or place of a society that has been marked by a large measure of political freedom, and that has not also used something comparable to a free market to organize the bulk of economic activity.[12]

The liberal economists value individual liberty so highly that they would defend markets even if it could be shown that they were not wholly efficient.

It must be emphasized that planning cannot get rid of uncertainty and because of this it cannot avoid making mistakes. It may however be able to disguise mistakes. There may be continuous full employment in a centrally planned economy, but one must also ask whether there is any element of coercion in the labour market, and whether workers are being employed producing goods that are not wanted. If unemployment is an absolute evil, then coercion and inefficiency may seem small prices to pay to avoid it; but the choice between economic systems must depend on how one values both economic and social objectives.

OPPOSITION TO THE MARKET

We have considered the liberal case, in which there is an *a priori* preference for markets, and the Keynesian approach, in which there are doubts about the ability of the economy to achieve full employment unaided. We now consider some objections to the market, beginning with those of our third group, the extreme left, who reject the whole neo-classical framework.

In the liberal tradition, individualism is both an assumption and a political value. It is assumed that individuals rationally and consistently pursue their own interests, and should be allowed and encouraged to act independently, free of the dominance of the state. The extreme left rejects both the assumption and the value. The assumption is rejected because the worker cannot act independently; he is the instrument of the capitalist. Individualism, which is an illusion in capitalist society anyway, destroys the true relations between men and between man and himself. Whether the market operates efficiently is not important; the major question is not planning versus the market but socialism versus capitalism.

Opinion is divided on whether the market will be used once capitalism has been abolished. Most, but not all, authors agree that consumer goods will be allocated through a market, but there are strong objections to its use in relation to production. For example, an editorial in the *Monthly Review* admonished Yugoslavia thus:

> The lesson which every socialist should take to heart and never tire of repeating is clear; it is necessary not only to abolish private property in the means of production but also production for profit. Beware of the market; it is Capitalism's secret weapon! Comprehensive planning is the heart and core of genuine socialism.[13]

The total Marxist rejection of market capitalism has influenced British left-wing thinking. The Labour Party, founded as a socialist but non-Marxist party, has generally objected to the market on less fundamental grounds, but at times some of its objections have been in sympathy with a Marxist approach.

The most deeply felt antipathy to the market is on ethical grounds: the system may be efficient but it is immoral. It appeals to man's basest instincts. The Labour Party manifesto, *Labour and the Nation*, spoke of the 'sordid struggle for private gain'. Then also, the market produces a distribution of income and wealth, and hence a pattern of goods, which reflects the whims of the rich rather than the needs of the general public. Bernard Shaw, typically acerbic, wrote '. . . a nation which cannot afford food and clothing for its children cannot be allowed to pass as wealthy because it has provided a pretty coffin for a dead dog.'[14] Such feelings persist, together with a fear that reliance on the market leads inevitably to unjust distribution[15] and a residual feeling that whatever the distribution of income, some expenditure is so frivolous that it ought to be discouraged.

The question of the efficiency of the market system becomes a moral one if, as appeared before the war, it is responsible for the misery of prolonged high unemployment. To the extreme left such events are no surprise, since they do not expect the market system to work efficiently. A favourite expression is the 'anarchy of the market' which seems to mean not only lack of overall direction but chaos. For example, in the *Anti-Dühring* Engels wrote: 'With this recognition, at last, of the real nature of the productive forces of today, the social anarchy of production gives place to a social regulation of production upon a definite plan, according to the needs of the community and of each individual.'[16]

The objection to the market partly inheres in the Marxist distinction between production for profit and production for use; but it is also felt that the market cannot be relied on to deliver the goods to anyone, not even the wealthy owners of deceased dogs. The inter-war period, still an important source of current attitudes, appeared to show that free markets do not work. In particular they had not ensured that resources, especially labour, were fully employed.

Objection to the market is not unique to the far left. There is an important general objection to the individualist basis of liberal economics. It is argued that the view of man as competitive and self-seeking is contrary to his true nature; that he seeks community and cooperation rather than conflict and solitary striving. The strains that competitive society places on its members are brilliantly described in Philip Slater's *The Pursuit of Loneliness*.[17]

It is difficult not to be sympathetic to such arguments, but the problem is what, in practice, is to replace markets. It is difficult to imagine a 'community' of sixty million people. The choice, unless there are fundamental changes in the organization of our society, is not between competition and community but between competition and central direction.

The man of moderate opinion draws his views, as we have said, partly from the work of Keynes, but they encompass more. Scepticism about markets extends not only to the overall behaviour of the economy but also to microeconomic questions. The sceptics typically reject, for example, the view that the solution to the housing problem would be to abolish interventions such as rent control and rely more on the free market. They assume that monopoly and imperfect competition are widespread features of economic life, and have severe doubts about the role of financial markets in allocating resources. These views are most typical of Keynes's colleagues and successors at Cambridge but they have a very wide currency.

A further source of influence on public opinion has been the work of Professor Galbraith, particularly *The Affluent Society*.[18] Although generally rejected by academic economists, that book and to a lesser degree his *The New Industrial State*[19] were acclaimed by those who were already repelled by the grosser aspects of market capitalism, and for whom his commentary struck many sympathetic chords. It is true that the United States have been notoriously poor in providing urban amenities. It does seem absurd that lavatory paper can be provided in every colour but that it is apparently impossible to provide an efficient or even a safe public transport system.

The two themes of Galbraith that are most relevant for the issue of planning are the assertion that advertising destroys consumer choice and that the development of large-scale production produces a general desire for economic planning because firms need assured conditions of supply and demand. (Advertising is also part of the attempt to control demand.)

Liberal economists think that Galbraith's analysis is faulty.[20] Advertising does not guarantee successful sales, as the long list of failures of heavily advertised products testifies (although liberal economists do recognize the dangers of uncontrolled advertising for medical products). And while companies using large-scale production will prefer stable market conditions, the market provides institutions for dealing with uncertainty and they are prepared to accept risks provided that the anticipated returns are large enough. The emphasis on uncertainty and the role of the government reducing it is subject to the comments already made about the government's ability to forecast the future. Whatever the objections, Galbraith has contributed to the feeling that markets cannot work and that planning is either necessary or inevitable.

Whatever the intellectual origins of doubts about the market, they are based on a humane concern for the public good. In the folk memory, 'the market' entails rotting slums, women and children in the mines, sewage in the streets and endless dole queues. Rejection of the market may mean steadily accelerating inflation and a stagnant economy, but that may seem a small price to pay to avoid such evils or their present-day equivalents. The claim that these fears are groundless, that either the diagnosis is wrong or that a solution can be found within the market system, is not believed. In addition, those involved in the actual process of government, as politicians or administrators, are interveners by nature and thus it is hardly surprising that the general view will be that the economy cannot safely be left to run itself.

At the moment the planning debate is once again open. The policy failures of recent years have cast serious doubts on the middle-of-the-road approach to economic policy based on overall demand management and scepticism about markets. Opinions have shifted. The government has expressed its own doubts about conventional policy and has admitted its own impotence. It has not sought additional powers to regulate the economy, nor has it suggested that greater reliance should be placed on market forces. The liberal call for less intervention has received some support, but the liberals have by no means captured the Conservative Party. Those who continue to press for Keynesian remedies usually add to them a call for permanent incomes policies and may urge import controls as a way of freeing ourselves from the constraints of our position as an open economy. The left makes stronger calls for planning and claims that it can get rid of unemployment by planning. It has found a new scapegoat in the multi-national companies, and argues for a new style of public ownership. On a world scale, the failure to recover rapidly from the slump of 1975 is producing calls for protection. It is all strikingly, even horrifyingly, reminiscent of the 1930s.

Chapter 3: Planning in the Thirties

The experiences of the 1930s cannot be ignored in a study of post-war economic policies. Harold Wilson was the first Prime Minister whose political career did not extend back to the thirties; his predecessors had formed their political beliefs in the thirties or even earlier. But, even where memories were not gained at first hand, their influence is still very potent: the dole queues of the thirties still haunt the corridors of Whitehall.

Pre-war history is particularly important for the Labour Party. Its sense of outrage at the workings of capitalism was fuelled by the thirties. Although it was then impotent politically, having been crushed by the aftermath of the 1931 crisis, the survivors, men such as Attlee, Cripps and Dalton, laid the foundations of post-war policy on their pre-war experiences.

I shall therefore present a brief outline of pre-war attitudes to planning as a prelude to post-war actions.

CONSERVATIVES AND PLANNING BEFORE THE WAR

Throughout this study, we come up against the problem that the Conservative Party is not a party of ideas. Both its supporters and its opponents agree about this. Richard Crossman remarked, not without a touch of envy, that 'the Conservatives can afford to rely on tradition and the leadership of men who are accepted as its interpreters. Indeed, Conservatism can be defined as whatever the Conservative leader says or does with the consent of his party.'[1] Nigel Harris, in his valuable guide to the Conservative Party, *Competition and the Corporate State*, puts it slightly differently: 'The aura of Conservatism must remain ambiguous, for intellectual clarity – that is, the clear expression of one set of interests before all others – is the enemy of co-operation between diverse groups.'[2]

An additional difficulty in analysing pre-war Conservatism lies in the fact that the Conservatives were usually the party in power. It is much easier to theorize about intentions than actions, and the socialists wrote extensively about their ideas on economic planning. The writing that did come from the Conservatives was mainly by those who were worried about the policies of the leadership.

In seeking to understand the Conservative Party's attitude to planning, both before and after the war, I shall adopt the conventional distinction between two strands of Conservatism: the Liberal-Conservative tradition and the Tory tradition. The distinction must be used with caution for the Conservative Party is a highly successful coalition and could not be so if there were two rigid factions. Cross-alliances on non-economic issues are common, and there is no clear division on economic issues. Further, the two strands of thought are not permanently linked to particular interest groups. Liberal-Conservatism, for example, with its origins in Peel's abolition of the Corn Laws, was associated with the triumph of commercial over landed interests. Disraeli, who fought Peel and gained the support of the shires, ended as a free trader himself. One enduring link has been between Liberal-Conservatism and the City; but the manufacturers have shifted between the two traditions according to where they believed their interests lay.

As far as attitudes to economic planning are concerned, the distinction that will be emphasized is the attitude to the role of the state in shaping society. As Lindsay and Harrington remark, 'Conservatism, as distinct from Toryism, has no real objectives.'[3] This aspect of Liberal-Conservatism has its intellectual ancestry in Burke's mistrust of rationality as a guide to human actions. Toryism, by contrast, has a picture of an ideal society. Thus it is more likely that Tories will propose radical departures in policy with a particular emphasis on intervention and a strong role for the state. They are more likely to be planners. Harold Macmillan, consistently, and Edward Heath, inconsistently, embody the Tory tradition. Churchill's views on economic policy embodied the Liberal-Conservative tradition. (He was, after all, driven from the Conservative Party for his support of free trade.)

In terms of rhetoric, the Tory tradition emphasizes unity and plays down conflict and competition. Disraeli's 'One Nation' symbolizes the basic idea. Corporatism (the belief in cooperation rather than competition as a means of solving economic and political issues) develops naturally from the Tory tradition since it is based on the idea of reasonable men combining to find rational solutions to the country's problems. The division between Liberal-Conservative and Tory does not lead to any simple predictions of attitudes to economic issues. On the question of social security, for example, the Liberal-Conservatives (and the Liberal Party) started by opposing any such interventions in the market but ended as pioneers of the Welfare State. At times appeals to liberal principles were barely disguised attempts to preserve the *status quo*. As Harris remarks, 'The principles which were supposed to guide Toryism and Liberalism dissolved in a purely opportunistic defence of those who held property.'[4]

In spite of the difficulty of tracing the traditions either in terms of particular ideas, or, even more, in terms of particular interest groups I shall adhere to the distinction, if only to emphasize that it is wrong to see the Conservative Party as embodying a single unified view of political philosophy or economic policy. It is particularly wrong to think of it as the party of laissez-faire. Since the 1930s, if not before, the Tory tradition has dominated the party. It is the brief flirtations with economic liberalism which have been uncharacteristic rather than the experiments with planning.

The Great Crash of 1929 and the subsequent events in the United Kingdom marked a turning point in Conservative Party history. Nigel Harris remarks: '1931 is a convenient point of time at which to identify the end of Liberal-Conservatism. For the end of free trade spelled the end of Liberalism.'[5] As David Winch said, 'Everywhere, the idea of the market as a sensitive, self-regulating mechanism for allocating resources suffered a setback, not only on the familiar grounds of equity but also of efficiency.'[6] It was no longer a choice between liberalism and corporatism but between two types of corporatism. Harris calls them *Étatiste* corporatism and pluralist corporatism. *Étatiste* corporatism was associated with the new industries such as the motor industry which used large-scale production. They were interested in state planning and welcomed the overall regulation of the economy to ensure stable markets for their output. They also employed a new type of skilled worker quite unlike the worker in the old craft traditions. Pluralist corporatism was associated with the older industries. They welcomed the creation of cartels (combinations of companies to agree on prices and market shares) and monopolies but expected them to be left to the control of businessmen.

CONSERVATIVE PLANNING

The policies of the National Government (which was predominantly Conservative) after 1931 were certainly described as planning at the time, and there was general agreement that planning was necessary. Evan Durbin, writing from the socialist side said: 'Indeed, in this country, planning has become one of the many subjects that scarcely enter into party controversy.' He reminded his readers:

> . . . it was the Conservative Party which passed the Electrical Supply Act of 1928, placed the London Passenger Transport Bill on the Statute Book, set up the Exchange Equalization Fund, has cartelized sections of the agricultural industry, is making some attempt to reorganize and unify the iron and steel industry, is subsidizing shipping, and proposes to begin the first stages of geographical planning.[7]

These extensions of the government's economic actions have been described by Samuel Beer as the foundation of the managed economy.[8] But ideas of management and planning were very different from those which prevailed after the war. The abandonment of the Gold Standard in 1931 allowed the government to adopt an expansionary monetary policy, but the significant features of planning were concerned with interference in particular markets rather than with overall regulation of the economy. The growth of large-scale industry and the development of monopolies at the best of times would have raised doubts about the unaided workings of competition. But these were not the best of times; the chronic problem of increased competition in Britain's export markets and the particular problems caused by the over-valued exchange rate after 1925 and the worldwide depression after 1929 all suggested that the solution was not to increase competition but to reduce it. Thus the typical policies of the period were the encouragement of cartels in domestic markets and eventually protection from foreign competition. (Keynes himself argued for protection after 1931.)

The policies of the National Government were thus those of 'pluralist corporatism', and did not imply a greatly increased role for the state. The most important criticism of Conservative Party policy came from the *Étatiste* corporatists; Harold Macmillan was the dominant figure, with Oliver Stanley and Robert Boothby as his main supporters. Macmillan described himself, in 1926, as one of the growing number of Conservatives who were becoming impatient of the doctrinaire laissez-faire attitude of the party as a whole. In 1927, he, Boothby, Stanley and J. Loder published *Industry and the State*. Macmillan saw it as

. . . a first essay in devising some coherent system, lying in between unadulterated private enterprise and collectivism. It was a policy which I afterwards called 'the Middle Way'; an industrial structure with the broad strategic control in the hands of the State and the tactical operation in the hands of private management, with public and private ownership operating side by side.[9]

Competition was seen as wasteful and destructive. The state should force amalgamations in order to speed 'the great world movement away from unfettered competition and the conditions of economic anarchy, which such competition now brings, towards federation, cooperation and combination.'[10] *The Middle Way*, published in 1938, marks the fullest development of Macmillan's pre-war ideas. 'In a sense,' as he later wrote, 'this was a plea for planned capitalism.' Its initial premiss was that all political parties had become conscious of something radically wrong with the economic system. He rejected the socialist approach because

> . . . even if their 'economic totalitarianism' would work without political tyranny, it would sacrifice the beneficial dynamic element that private enterprise can give to society when exercised in its proper sphere, and because it would not provide the scope for human diversity which is essential if men are really to be free.[11]

His proposals included the state control of all investment, state subsidies and investment in industry, manipulation of interest rates, deficit financing and the nationalization of the Bank of England. Macmillan was a backbencher throughout the period; his views were not generally accepted by the pre-war Conservative Party, but apart from state control of investment, they became the policy of first the Labour and then of the Conservative governments. He proposed planned capitalism because he thought it was the only way of saving democracy. By the time the Conservative Party regained power in 1951, there appeared to be a solution which, while extending the responsibility of the state, did not call for a great expansion of its powers and which could encourage competition in industry without the fear that it would cause unemployment. By the time that Macmillan himself came to power, the overwhelming problem, which he attempted to solve in the Tory planning tradition, was not unemployment but inflation.

THE LABOUR PARTY

The Labour Party held office for two brief periods before the war, each time as a minority government. It produced no initiatives in economic policy and its financial policy was completely orthodox. After the débâcle of 1931, neither the Labour Party nor the trade union movement had any influence on policy. The period is however important for the effect it had on the development of the Labour Party's ideas.

In some ways the continuity of those ideas seems remarkable. The Labour Party's manifesto of 1918, *Labour and the New Social Order*, set out the basic programme which was to be presented twenty-seven years later in the manifesto of 1945, *Let Us Face the Future*. That programme was carried out almost to the letter by the Labour Government of 1945–51. This apparent thirty-year continuity of policy, adopted by what Samuel Beer has called the Socialist Generation, concealed important shifts in the party's ideas. These were shifts in its political and economic analysis, in particular of public ownership, which were inextricably linked with a changed attitude to planning. Keynes was a key influence but his ideas were not to be generally accepted until the end of the war.

When the Labour Party was founded, it had adopted a non-Marxist socialist creed and was committed to social ownership. Its attitude to planning was part of this commitment, as can be seen in *Labour and the New Social Order* (1918). Among the demands of the Labour Party were:

... a genuinely scientific re-organization of the nation's industry, no longer deflected by individual profiteering, on the basis of the Common Ownership of the Means of Production; the equitable sharing of the proceeds among all who participate in any capacity and only among those, and the adoption in particular services and occupations of those systems and methods of administration and control that may be found, in practice, best to promote, not profiteering, but the public interest.

Not surprisingly, since its author was Sidney Webb, it was full of optimistic Fabianism with its references to 'scientific' 'systems and methods of administration'. It also illustrates the ways in which the Labour Party rejected market capitalism: 'promotion of the public interest' is contrasted with 'profiteering' and there is emphasis on the equitable sharing of income.

The neo-classical distinction between economic efficiency and equity was irrelevant. Since capitalism could not be equitable there was no point in finding whether it could be efficient. Private capitalism was to be replaced by planned socialism, for, as the Labour Party pamphlet of 1934, *For Socialism and Peace*, argued,

> There is no halfway house between a society based on private ownership of the means of production with the profit of the few as the measure of success, and a society where public ownership of those means enables the resources of the nation to be deliberately planned for attaining the maximum of general wellbeing.

Social ownership was proposed as the solution to the economic and political injustices that the Labour Party was pledged to remove. Originally, capitalism was rejected as an economic and moral system. But during the inter-war years, the attack on capitalism concentrated on unemployment, which provided the foundation of the Labour Party case for planned socialism. The depression was the most evident example of the breakdown of capitalism, the most blatant demonstration of its irrationality. In Attlee's words:

> I believe that it is impossible to contend against the tendencies which are making every day for a planned society, and which render it out of the question to continue a class society based on gross inequalities of wealth. Capitalism is manifestly failing. A temporary recovery from depression gives it a short new lease of life, but the next depression is deeper than its predecessor.[12]

Attlee spoke of the Labour Party's intention '. . . to substitute for the anarchy of competitive industrialism a planned and organized system . . .'[13]

A number of explanations for the prolonged unemployment were put forward. Some were in the Marxist tradition and saw unemployment as a deliberate and inevitable part of capitalist exploitation. Other writers, for example G. D. H. Cole, used more traditional analysis and blamed the growth of monopoly. According to some, high unemployment was deliberate; according to others, it was due to capitalist mistakes. In either case, the obvious solution seemed to be to take over private enterprise and introduce planning to ensure that goods produced would be sold, that machines would not stand idle, and that all who wanted to work would be able to do so.

The idea of planning in the public interest was contrasted with Conservative policies which were seen as planning in the interests of capitalists. For example, Cole:

There has been a great deal of so-called 'planning' during the last few years under the auspices of the National Government; but nearly all of it has been planning for scarcity and not for plenty. The Government has 'planned' for dearness and for the profit of capitalists, not for the well-being of the mass of ordinary people.[14]

The emphasis on investment as the main cause of economic cycles became more widely accepted as Keynes's early ideas began to influence socialist thought. Blame was placed on the banking system, which was accused of making credit too readily available during booms and too tight during the depression. These ideas strengthened the Labour Party's traditional hostility, still evident today, towards financial institutions. Control of the banks, or at least of the Bank of England, was seen as an essential part of planning.

However, under the influence of Keynes's later writing, emphasis moved away from credit and investment to savings and investment. In *The Coming Struggle for Power*, John Strachey, who became Minister for War in the first post-war government, made it his main explanation of the economic cycle:

For it is now agreed, as we have seen, that the price-level

moves whenever investment ceases to equal savings, and that investment does constantly differ from savings because quite different and unrelated people do the investing and the saving, and do them without reference to each other's actions.[15]

Strachey's concern with price rather than output changes was derived from the formal analysis of Keynes's *Treatise on Money*, but his real concern was with the cycle of output. He rejected Keynes's suggestion that the solution was to vary interest rates, and called for the abolition of capitalism:

It has now been in effect admitted by the leading capitalist economists themselves, that the true cause of the periodic breakdowns of their system is the planlessness with which production is undertaken. Nor can this state of things be altered so long as capitalism endures.[16]

Thus Keynes's new ideas on the causes of unemployment seemed to strengthen the Labour Party's case for planning. Unemployment was caused by a mismatching of decisions on savings and investment; the problem could be solved by controlling investment directly. Planned socialism was the obvious answer. But Keynes himself was to sabotage the argument. He argued that overall demand management, within the competitive capitalist system, could solve the problem, and the post-war years seemed to show that he was right.

CONCLUSIONS

The Labour Party was swept into power after the Second World War. By contrast with the Conservatives who were given six years to adapt their policies to the changed post-war conditions, the Labour Party had only its wartime experiences in the Coalition Government and its pre-war traditions to guide it. Those traditions were based first on the commitment to social ownership embodied in the 1918 manifesto, and then on its outrage at the unemployment of the thirties. The commitment to social ownership was based partly on its rejection of the market ethic, on its anger at the unequal distribution of income and wealth, and on the high costs in terms of human suffering of the remnants of laissez-faire. Its solution was to replace the market by planning. The commitment to planning seemed to be strengthened by the prolonged high unemployment of the thirties. It was seen as the strongest evidence that market capitalism could not work. The post-war Labour Government duly introduced planning; but the experiment was soon abandoned.

Chapter 4: The Post-war Labour Government and Planning

THE FIRST ECONOMIC SURVEY

The first post-war Labour Government came to power at a time which was particularly favourable to the introduction of planning. Planning was generally believed to have worked both efficiently and equitably during the war. Unlike the period after the First World War, no one was proposing a rapid return to free market conditions. The Labour Party was committed to planning, and, confident that it would receive support, launched the first major planning experiment. Its history can be gleaned from the successive versions of the *Economic Survey*, starting in 1947.[1] They show how economic planning – that is, the attempt to achieve targets for the pattern and scale of industrial development – was replaced by demand management. By 1951 planning had more or less been abandoned. Welfare capitalism replaced socialism as the Labour Party's political objective. It combined Keynesian methods of demand management – using general rather than specific measures to influence the economy – with the extension of the Welfare State. The Labour Party could no longer rely on electoral support for planning, and the Conservatives, partly in response to popular sentiment, briefly moved towards Liberal-Conservatism. The Conservatives came to power in 1951 claiming to 'set the people free'; but in practice they adopted policies which were barely distinguishable from those of the defeated Labour Government.

Since national economic planning was a new venture, the first *Survey* devoted some space to defining the object of planning – 'to use the national resources in the best interests of the nation as a whole' – and to providing it with a philosophy:

There is an essential difference between totalitarian and democratic planning. The former subordinates all individual desires and preferences to the demands of the state. . . . But in normal times, the people of a democratic country will not give up their freedom of choice to their government. A democratic government must, therefore, conduct its economic planning in a manner which preserves the maximum possible freedom of choice to the individual citizen.

This formed the essence of speeches made by ministers round the country. Stafford Cripps, for example, said in March 1947:

You can persuade, encourage, inspire, but you cannot compel. And even if it were possible, it would be undesirable. That is why the plan we have put forward is fundamentally based on the understanding cooperation of both sides of industry – and it must be of both sides.[2]

He continued in characteristic vein: 'For a time we must submerge all thought of personal gain and personal ambition in the greater and deeper desire to give our all to secure the future prosperity and happiness of our people.'[3] Douglas Jay wrote in *Labour's Plan for 1947*, a popular account of the *Survey*,

The targets for the end of 1947 are not, of course, rigid orders, to be followed out, as in the military sense, by compulsion. They are objectives, which the government thinks should be reached, and can be reached, through a joint effort, by the public and the government together.[4]

The type of planning introduced by the *Survey* had to satisfy those Labour supporters who were firm believers in planning and allay the fears of those who feared that planning meant coercion (the early post-war enthusiasm for our Russian allies had evaporated) or a return to wartime stringency. The government had to be seen to be planning, but it was clearer what peacetime planning could not be than what it could be. Herbert Morrison, who as Lord President of the Council was responsible for economic planning, had described the new approach in terms that were as stirring in general as they were vague in particular:

> . . . planning as it is taking shape in this country under our eyes is something new and constructively revolutionary, which will, I think, be regarded in times to come as a contribution to civilization as vital and as distinctively British as parliamentary democracy and the rule of law.'[5]

The fact that planning had been accepted during the war and that the administrative machinery for it had been established did not, in spite of its help in providing a favourable initial reception, prove much of an advantage in the end. The problems were very different. In wartime there is general agreement on the overall objective – 'the concentration of the nation's maximum effort against the enemy, so as to bring the fullest possible force to bear upon him at the appropriate moments within the period of hostilities.'[6] People are prepared to make major sacrifices, including temporary restrictions on individual freedom, when national survival is at stake. Also, the economic problems associated with war are exceptional. Large shifts in resources are required; men and women are needed in the forces; industry has to shift to arms production; sources of supply may be cut off. Even the most ardent supporters of markets will be reluctant to rely on the price system alone to achieve such rapid changes in market structure. Even if it operated efficiently, the short-run effects on the distribution of income and wealth can be both dramatic and undesirable (producing the much-pilloried 'War Profiteers' of the First World War). In peace there is no such simple agreed objective, and constraints on freedom are soon resented.

The Labour Government recognized these difficulties but had no better guide to the problem of planning in peacetime than its wartime experience and pre-war political tradition. The two influences can be traced in *The Old World and the New Society*, which was presented to the

Annual Conference of 1942. The commitment to planning was clear: 'The basis of our democracy must be planned production for community use . . . A planned society must replace the old competitive system . . . We have learned in the war that the anarchy of private competition must give way to ordered planning under national control.'[7]

On the basis of the report, the annual conference of May 1942 passed a resolution entitled 'A Planned Economic Democracy'. It said, '. . . there must be no return after the war to an unplanned competitive society, which inevitably produces economic insecurity, industrial inefficiency and social inequality.'

By 1947 the confidence in planning had waned. The 1945 election manifesto, *Let Us Face the Future*, had made only passing references to planning, mainly in relation to investment. In the immediate post-war years, the main problem of economic policy had been the dismantling of the war economy. The first *Economic Survey* could look ahead to more normal days, but the problems associated with the aftermath of the war still dominated the outlook. It listed the major objectives as increasing exports to pay for imports, and expanding the basic industries and services, particularly coal and power. (In the winter of 1947, coal shortages had caused widespread shutdown of industry.)

The style of planning described in the *Survey* to meet these objectives reflected the techniques developed during the war. There were three official working parties – on manpower, on investment, and on imports and the balance of payments. They produced trial balance sheets designed to indicate gaps between resources and demand. Planning was used to close those gaps 'in the way most advantageous to the national interest.'[8] This technique was exactly parallel to the wartime approach. By the end of the war, manpower was the main resource problem, and this emphasis was also found in the *Economic Survey*. Douglas Jay emphasized the role of the 'Manpower Budget' in *Labour's Plan for 1947*: 'The essence of this plan is the "Manpower Budget" by which the resources of the nation are marshalled and allocated, not in the old-fashioned financial terms, but in terms of actual men and women.'

The aspiration was admirable, but since the direction of labour had been abandoned it was unclear how the desired allocation was to be achieved. The *Survey* set out manpower targets – the coal industry ('Expansion of the coal-mining labour force is priority number one') needed 40,000 extra workers; textile and clothing needed 70,000, etcetera – but was vague on how they would be met. ('It is a framework, not a blueprint.') The manpower estimates were 'neither an ideal distribution, nor a forecast of what will happen.' The implications of the plan were to be discussed with the representatives of both sides of industry 'in order to develop the best possible means of carrying it out.'

The mixture of pre-war tradition and wartime experience could be seen in the *Survey*'s assumption that the allocation of resources could not be left solely to market forces, and that scarcity could not be allowed to lead to high prices:

Economic budgets must be balanced by measures to increase resources or to curtail requirements. Otherwise, less essentials will push essentials out of the queue. Too many luxuries will be produced and not enough food and clothes and coal; too many toys and not enough children's boots; too many greyhound tracks, and not enough houses; too much consumption and not enough exports to buy our essential imports.

The note of austerity and disapproval of 'luxury' expenditure was also sounded in Jay's pamphlet. He recorded that recruitment into 'luxury industries, such as football pools' would be limited, and that certain public sports would be limited to weekends.

The *Economic Survey* was concerned almost entirely with the discussion of output and manpower needs. Only 2 out of 141 paragraphs were concerned with examination of total national income. They included a table which set out the proportions of national income to be allocated to the main items of expenditure. There was no indication of what the size of total output would be, nor whether such an allocation of resources would cause problems of demand management.

To meet its objectives the government could employ a small residue of direct controls left over from the war, of which the most important was building licences. In addition, about one-third of consumption was still subject to rationing. It was also able to exercise some control over labour allocation. Given the lack of effective instruments, it is hardly surprising that the plan, which called for quite significant changes in the structure of output, was not very successful. The *Economic Survey* for 1948 reviewed the performance for the past year. The balance of payments was far worse than expected. Steel and coal production were both below target, though not seriously. Housing was a long way below target, largely because of bad weather and shortage of raw materials. As far as the manpower budget was concerned, total civilian employment was 330,000 more than expected. Even so, the coal industry and the textile industry did not get as much labour as had been planned. The big, unplanned increases were in distribution and consumer services.

The first *Economic Survey* was recognizably a plan in that the government set the objectives for the development of the economy in quantitative terms; but it did not provide itself with the instruments necessary to counteract market forces; its philosophy of democratic planning did not allow it to do so. Nor did it meet two further objectives proposed by Morrison. It did not show how the growth of productivity might be increased, and it did not look further ahead than one year. The first objective remains a chimera; the second was at least achieved in the Labour Government's Long-term Programme of 1948.

The rather confused approach to planning displayed in the first *Economic Survey* must at least partly be attributed to the role played by Herbert Morrison. As B. Donoughue and G. W. Jones show in their biography,[9] Morrison was a devoted planner who liked the sense of order and the personal authority that it provided. But he became hostile to the Russian example of full socialist planning and increasingly pragmatic and attached to the idea of a mixed economy. He lacked 'a flair, a feel, and a developed instinct for economic decisions.'[10]

His problems were increased by the hostility of the Treasury, without which planning could not work. To start with, the Treasury was excluded from the planning process, but the Lord President's Office could not operate successfully without their support. Then the Treasury, according to Donoughue and Jones, treated the Lord President's Office in the way in which, many years later, they were to be accused of treating the Department of Economic Affairs. 'Demotion, fragmentation, violation and ultimately elimination, were the stages by which the Lord President's independent powers were whittled away and the Treasury was re-established in its primacy.[11]

THE 1948 SURVEY

The *Economic Survey* of 1948 was overshadowed by the publication in December of that year of the Long-term Programme. It did, however, include some important guides to the development of official attitudes to planning.

In November 1947, on the resignation of Hugh Dalton, Stafford Cripps became Chancellor of the Exchequer while retaining his responsibilities as Minister for Economic Affairs. This gave him great power: as Christopher Dow remarked, 'It is probably true that no minister before or since, even during the war years, had as great power to direct the economy as Sir Stafford Cripps.'[12] It also restored the Treasury, which had lost importance during the war, to its position at the centre of economic management.

This combining under one head of the Treasury and the Minister of Economic Affairs made the *Economic Survey* for 1948[13] a very different document from its predecessor. There was less rhetoric and philosophy, but a much more complex analysis of the overall problem of demand management.

Part of the change in tone was due to the experiences of 1947. Convertibility of sterling (which allowed the free exchange of sterling for dollars) had been tried and abandoned. World prices of food and raw materials had risen violently. It was not known whether or not an American loan would be forthcoming. An appendix to the *Survey* looked back to 1947 and pointed to the lessons for the future.

Perhaps the outstanding lesson of the experiment hitherto made in democratic planning in this country, apart from the limitations imposed by dependence on foreign trade, is the importance of the voluntary cooperation of the individual with the plan set by the central authorities. In the matter of industrial productivity, for instance, the government can encourage, but it cannot compel.

The main national objective in 1948 was the 'restoration of external stability, and the narrowing of the gap in our trade with the Western Hemisphere, and, above all, with the dollar countries. The whole of the government's planning will be strenuously devoted to this aim . . .'

The most interesting feature of the *Survey* was a table showing the total resources available to meet expenditure demands. It also provided a very open discussion of the possibility that there would be excess demand in the economy; gave an estimate of the required level of private saving if inflationary pressure were to be avoided; and warned of the consequences of inadequate voluntary savings.

If the level of savings, which people would choose of their own accord to make, falls far short of that required by the planned total of investment, the balance can be restored only in two ways – or in a combination of the two. The capital development programmes or the export targets may fail to be achieved. Otherwise, prices and costs will be driven up. The total incomes of a large part of the nation will be reduced. Those who are in a position to exploit the market will make abnormal profits. To the extent that these are not spent within the year, savings will be increased. A balance will be restored, but at inflated prices. The cost will be a strain on the working of the economic controls, a partial failure of plans, and a burden on all those whose incomes lag behind prices.

The *Economic Survey* for 1948 presents a useful guide to the stage that economic policy had reached. There was thought to be a desperate need to restore the balance of payments, and a fear that there might be acute shortages of raw materials. There was a severe risk of rapid inflation. The instruments used to avoid it were rationing and controls to deflect demand from consumption and investment, and price and wage restraint to control inflation directly. At the same time there was an attempt to use budgetary policy along Keynesian lines to reduce the overall level of demand. It was not yet central to economic policy but its role was beginning to be understood.

LONGER-TERM PLANNING

In March 1947, Cripps announced the establishment of a Central Planning Staff, headed by the Chief Planning Officer. It was to be advised by an independent board of people from both sides of industry. Its first major task became the preparation of a Long-term Programme to be submitted to the Organization for European Economic Cooperation as part of the conditions for Marshall Aid, the United States aid to Europe after World War II. All member countries of OEEC (now OECD) were invited to submit a plan showing how they would obviate the need for aid by mid-1952. Britain's plan, the Long-term Programme, covering the years 1948 to 1952, was submitted to the OEEC in 1948, and published as a White Paper in December of that year.[14]

Its comments on the nature of planning are revealing, since they show how Britain explained itself to foreigners, rather than how it exhorted its own citizens:

Economic planning in the United Kingdom is based

upon three fundamental facts: the economic fact that the United Kingdom economy must be heavily dependent upon international trade; the political fact that it is, and intends to remain, a democratic nation, with a high degree of individual liberty; and the administrative fact that no economic planning body can be aware (or indeed ever could be aware) of more than the very general trends of future economic developments.

The government argued that, given the uncertainty of economic developments, the long-term plans must be kept flexible. 'A persistent adherence to targets or time-tables based on assumptions, which have been falsified by events, might well be as disastrous as leaving the whole matter to chance.' It also argued that our democratic traditions must severely limit the chosen methods of planning.

Finally, recovery must not be bought at the price of arbitrary and excessive interference with the rights of the individual. The United Kingdom intends to make resolute use of its traditional techniques of financial policy and of the direct public control of certain basic industries. A large measure of control will have to be retained over imports, over the total amount of home consumption, and over the scale and composition of investment. But powers of prohibition and compulsion, though they must be used to set limits to economic freedom, must not be allowed except in very special circumstances to infringe the personal freedom of the individual. The execution, as well as the preparation of plans, must be based upon the willing cooperation and understanding of the general public.

The Long-term Programme was therefore to be no more and no less than a statement of economic strategy; it was not a 'rigid set of instructions for several years ahead'.

In 1947, when the Planning Staff was established, there were four major objectives: the achievement of the balance of payments target without deflating the economy, the restoration and expansion of capital equipment, the restoration of consumption to pre-war levels and the establishment of an efficient and smoothly working economic system in which incentives to produce and consume would operate with the minimum of control and compulsion.

The Staff made a long-term survey whose function was to identify the problems, to see what was involved in their solution, to see what structural changes were required, to ensure that ordinary economic incentives were helping to achieve the solution, and finally, to see how government resources could best be deployed. 'In one sense,' as Austin Robinson said, 'we were engaged in what has since come to be called "indicative planning".'[15] Robinson emphasized that the plan required adequate instruments; it was no use creating a list of objectives and just hoping that they would come about. The instruments available to the planners included controls over investment programmes via the Investment Programmes Committee, and building licences and controls. In addition budgetary policy became a deliberate instrument of overall demand management, and was particularly used to support the investment programme. Finally there was some residual power to direct manpower. Robinson's conclusions were that until 1950 'it was possible not only to plan, but also to achieve a structural readjustment of the economy'.

How successful was the Long-term Programme? There are really two separate questions: Were the targets achieved? How far was this due to planning? Joan Mitchell provides a detailed answer to the first question in *Groundwork to Economic Planning*.[16] As she says, 'In broad outline and in considerable detail, the Programme was undoubtedly achieved by 1952–53, at least in the sense that it was a good forecast'.[17] The balance of payments was close to forecast, total production reached the Programme level and individual industrial targets were generally achieved.

On the question of the role of planning in achieving the Programme's objectives, Dr Mitchell offers an extremely cautious conclusion. 'At the very least, it can be said that the evidence does not show any *prima facie* case for the anti-planners or the cynics.'[18]

One feature that makes it difficult to assess the success of the Programme, but which also casts some doubt on its importance, is that it played virtually no part in public discussion of economic policy. 'What happened to the Programme after its publication in December 1948 was – on the face of it – almost nothing. Nothing, in that after some description of it in the Economic Survey for 1949, the Long-term Programme as such was put away to collect dust quite quickly by Ministers and officials alike.'[19] As Dr Mitchell explains, there were a number of good reasons for this. OEEC was unable to agree on a coherent general programme. Britain was soon faced with the sterling problems which led to devaluation in 1949. The Korean War started in 1950. Finally, the Labour Government was replaced in 1951 by a Conservative Government hostile to planning.

In spite of Dr Mitchell's modest conclusion and the pall of silence which seemed to have covered the Programme, Robinson's comments suggest that the Long-term Programme was successful, both as an early example of an indicative plan and as an attempt to speed structural change by means of direct controls. This is not to say that the market system might not have done better; but given that the government feared the inflationary and distributional effects of reliance on market forces, while some resources were extremely scarce, it was a successful exercise.

FROM PLANNING TO DEMAND MANAGEMENT

The final three *Economic Surveys* proposed by the Labour Government illustrated the evolution from the idea of national planning (even if only for one year ahead) to the idea of demand management by means of fiscal policy. The word 'planning' was much more rarely used, being replaced by 'plans' (a much milder concept than planning) and 'forecasts'. In addition, the balance of the *Surveys* changed with an even greater share being taken by discussion of national income forecasts and the problems of demand management.

The *Economic Survey* for 1949[20] could look back on 'a year of great and steady progress'. The previous survey had been based on the assumption that American aid would not be provided. The aid was in the event generously provided; it meant that output was not held back by shortages of raw materials, and industrial production arose by 12 per cent. This growth of output eased many problems. 'It permitted exports to rise faster than imports, without total national resources being reduced; it allowed investment to increase, and it allowed an appreciable improvement in consumption.' This success had been achieved without aggravating inflationary pressure. This was explained partly by the government's fiscal policy – there had been a large budget surplus – and partly by the voluntary restraints on wages and prices.

The outlook for 1949 did not anticipate increases in output of anything approaching those achieved in 1948. The dominant problem, again, was expected to be the dollar shortage. The discussion of the outlook was generally much more tentative. Industrial output was discussed only in terms of coal, electricity, steel, other raw materials, textiles and agriculture. The figures were presented either in terms of what was desirable or what was feasible, but there was little sense of directed effort.

In its discussion of manpower, the *Survey* claimed that its policy for 1948 had met with a large measure of success. 'The Control of Engagement Order was effective in enabling large numbers of workers to be guided into essential work during 1948, without the interference with individual freedom which the widespread use of powers of direction would entail.'

The discussion of the national income forecasts again concentrated on the problems of inflation. In spite of the rapid growth of output between 1947 and 1948, consumption had only risen by $\frac{1}{2}$ per cent. Although the government attributed this largely to its budgetary policy, it also feared that there may have been some frustrated demand.

For 1949, it clearly felt that there could be no possibility of reducing the tax burden.

The *Survey* ended with an account of the tasks for 1949. It read like a cross between a sermon and a call to arms: 'We must make a further effort [to expand US sales] . . . We must continue our exertions [to expand output] . . . We must seek continuously [to bring down costs] . . . The battle against inflation . . . must be fought . . .' The discussion of inflation was particularly pious:

> At home [inflation] strains the controls designed to secure 'fair shares' of scarce essential goods, and gives the black market operator the chance he seeks. Above all, a situation in which there is 'a lot of money about', and profits are easy to come by, lessens initiative and slackens the incentive to increase productivity.

The concluding sentences of the *Survey* are significant:

> The policies we must follow are no longer the transition policies of re-adjustment from time of war or the improvisations of crisis. They are becoming rather the steady policies of long-term progress. With the continued understanding and cooperation of the whole community, the government is confident that these policies can succeed.

The ambitions of planning and the instruments used to achieve them thus became firmly identified with transitional problems. They were not expected to play a central role once normal life had been restored.

The *Economic Survey* for 1950[21] was described by *The Economist* as 'meek almost to the point of being meaningless'. The main element of the outlook would be a continuation of deflationary policies. On productivity the *Survey* said: 'No specific target is set for productivity. We require and should seek to achieve the greatest possible increases in output per head.' The balance of payments was expected to remain the central economic problem, but 'It is particularly difficult to forecast how much progress will be made in 1950. . . .'

The *Economic Survey* referred back to the Long-term Programme and showed that considerable progress had been made in achieving its objectives. But the future role of the government was apparently to be limited to the general task of constraining demand at home to avoid the inflationary impact of the required improvement in the balance of trade.

The *Economic Survey* for 1951[22] was rather different from the other *Surveys*. It was a document prepared to meet the crisis caused by the upheaval of world markets due to the Korean War and the British decision to rearm. Thus the central problem was that of switching resources to the defence industry and of avoiding the excess demand likely to be associated with rapid rearmament. It is significant that despite the government's view that half a million additional defence workers would be needed by 1953-4, the *Economic Survey* contained no industrial manpower budgets. Although the government reintroduced certain controls, particularly of imports and prices, the transfer from manpower budgeting to fiscal budgeting was complete.

THE RETREAT FROM PLANNING

The political record of the 1945–51 Labour Government has been widely described and debated: to some it represents the party's finest hour; to others the great betrayal of the British working class. In any case, it carried out the programme of its election manifesto, *Let Us Face the Future* while abandoning the attempt to plan the economy. The programme outlined in *Let Us Face the Future* became both the first and the last step on the road to the promised land of the socialist commonwealth. Why did it change its mind?

I have emphasized the links between belief in socialism and belief in planning. In pre-war and early post-war Labour Party thought, they stood or fell together. If people found that planning was impossible and unnecessary, they lost faith in socialism: if they lost faith in socialism, they lost interest in planning. Both processes were at work, and they reinforced each other.

One view on the abandonment of planning, strongly argued by Samuel Beer, is that the trade union movement was never truly committed to socialism, and that once it could achieve its objectives by other means, it no longer supported socialism or planning, and that this was crucial. Further, Beer claims that the trade union movement destroyed planning by its refusal to surrender the right to free collective bargaining. At the foundation of the Labour Party, Arthur Henderson desired (according to Samuel Beer) a distinctive political creed to mark the end of the Labour–Liberal alliance. 'The adoption of socialism as an ideology was functional to this choice of political independence. If the party was to pursue power independently, it needed a set of beliefs and values, distinguishing it from other parties.'[23] Seen in these terms, the adoption of socialism is a major act of political opportunism – an act which could hardly on the common-sense view have sustained the Labour Party for the years between 1918 and 1945. Beer admits that there were valid reasons for the shift to the left, particularly by the trade unions. They had seen a great increase in their power during the First World War, and had reaped considerable benefit from the Liberal Government of 1906–18. But they recognized that while the Liberal Party was prepared to represent the interests of the working class, it was not prepared to give it power. Socialism provided a claim for political power for the unions in their own right. 'A class – or more precisely, the organized section of a class – was asserting its claim to power.'[24]

The unions did indeed gain immense power during the Second World War, helped by Bevin's ability to achieve great influence as a minister without losing his dominant position in the union movement. They maintained that power in the conditions of labour shortage after 1945. Further, they realized that they could maintain power under any government and did not need to commit themselves fully to one party or creed, even if their support naturally went to the Labour Party.

If the unions had gained so much power, why did they not use it to bring about socialism? The question must remain unresolved. The gap between those who argue that the unions did not want socialism and those who consider that they were cheated out of it (and continue to be cheated out of it) by the forces of capitalism is too wide to be closed by this discussion. Some evidence of trade union views was provided by the major TUC document on post-war economic policy, the *Interim Report*, published in 1944 and approved at that year's Congress.[25]

This announced in its Foreword, 'The Trade Union movement has long held the view that the existing forms of industrial and economic organization are not suited, if they ever were intended, to promote such aims as social security and full employment.' Its proposals were not extreme. The objectives of the trade union movement – the maintenance and improvement of wages, hours and conditions of labour, full employment and participation in management – could only be achieved within a system of public control. Public control would include the following: land and natural resources, the supply and availability of cash and credit, the rate of gross investment and the supply of capital for investment, the location of industry and physical planning, foreign trade and foreign lending and investment.

As far as planning was concerned the main emphasis was on investment. It was essential that there should be 'comprehensive planning of all large-scale investment, public and private, according to certain national and social priorities.' Planning was to be the responsibility of a National Investment Board which would survey, plan and lend. It would survey how much investment should be taken by the country as a whole, it would provide expert guidance over all schemes of long-term investment with a particular concern for full employment and price stability, and it would provide the finance.

The concern with investment was consistent with pre-war theories (notably those of Keynes) of the causes of unemployment. Planning and public ownership were proposed as the means to attain traditional trade union objectives. The proposals were pragmatic rather than doctrinaire; they could reasonably be amended if the objectives could be achieved by other means.

Beer's view that the trade unions' insistence on retaining free collective bargaining dealt the death-blow to planning cannot be established. It may be true that planning is incompatible with free collective bargaining, but it is not obviously so. The state can plan for a particular pattern of output and then use market forces to direct labour where it is needed. The resulting distribution of income may be undesirable on ethical grounds, or it may produce a pattern of demand which calls for considerable intervention in the market for consumer goods, but that is a different matter.

Planning is not inconsistent with a free labour market. The truth must be that 'collective bargaining' does not mean a free labour market, but means TUC control over the structure of pay. If that is so, the TUC can frustrate planning if at the same time it rules out labour direction. But the case is still not proven: we would need to find instances in which the Labour Government's desire to plan was clearly frustrated by the trade union movement. In fact the Labour Government was itself losing interest in planning, and it is this which needs to be explained.

The leadership's enthusiasm for socialism was waning. Paul Addison argues that although Attlee's ethics led him to believe in the Socialist Commonwealth, practical experience led him to believe in reformed capitalism. It did appear after all that major advances in the material welfare of the workers could be achieved under the capitalist system. 'The warm currents of social security and full employment began to melt the icy layers of anti-capitalist principle.'[26] The same thing seems to have happened to Cripps. Beer argues that Cripps was a committed planner throughout his life. That was true, but it was not a type of planning that rested on social ownership or on the direction of manpower. He saw in both wars how private enterprise could be made to serve the public interest, and towards the

75

end of his life he came to believe that if those responsible for the management of industry conformed to an ethic of high morality, the ends of Christian democracy could be served. Such a sentiment was typical of him. Morrison, a key figure in determining the approach to domestic policy, was never a doctrinaire socialist and was never able to form a coherent view of what peacetime planning could or should be.

Was the abandonment of planning a betrayal of pre-war promises? The key fact is surely that it looked as if full employment and improvements in welfare could be achieved without it. If so, there were very good reasons, in an avowedly democratic party, for abandoning it. Before the war, the experience of unemployment had led to the reasonable conclusion that the way to avoid it was to plan production and demand in detail so that they were equal. Machines would not be built unless there was a sure demand for their output. Production would be planned so that all workers would be employed. For the Labour Party it was natural to argue that if the planning was to be done in the interests of the workers, the ownership of capital should be transferred to the state.

But Keynes demonstrated that detailed planning was unnecessary and that full employment could be achieved under capitalism provided the government intervened to manage the overall level of demand. Whether or not he was right, the problems of the post-war British economy led to shortages of labour rather than to unemployment. Having had the plank of unemployment knocked from the planning platform, the Labour Party was left with its claim that resources should be used in the interests of the public rather than the capitalists. But a combination of taxation and welfare expenditure seemed to be achieving that. Attempts to plan the economy in any fuller sense led to insurmountable difficulties. How was the state to discover the nature of the public interest? The tendency of the Labour Government was to see it in terms of the austere personal standards set by Attlee and Cripps. That was, at any rate, what the public thought the government was doing. Having discovered the public interest, how was the government to direct resources in the required way? We have seen how conscious it was of the need to assure the public that it wanted to use cooperation, not coercion; but why should the public cooperate to produce a pattern of output it did not want? The problems which before the war had so clearly seemed to call for planned socialism did not reappear; planning was neither necessary nor desirable.

The government's retreat from planning did not go completely unopposed. In 1947, for example, Richard Crossman, Michael Foot and Ian Mikardo published *Keep Left*.[27] It appeared when the British were living in the midst of a coal crisis, a food crisis, a raw materials crisis, a manpower crisis, a trade crisis and a dollar crisis. Prominent among the list of '20 Things to Do Now' was the establishment of overall economic planning. They proposed that the central planning authority should be turned into a full-scale Ministry of Economic Affairs with a high-level minister free from other duties. They also argued for a more effective use of direct controls.

The strongest opposition to the retreat from socialism and planning came from Aneurin Bevan. The story was to continue after 1951, with Bevan's clashes first with Morrison and then with Gaitskell. The specific issue might be nationalization, but for Bevan the general issue was the nature of socialism and its necessary role in Labour Party policies. He was a committed planner (he acknowledged that economic planning was his 'King Charles's head'); but it was part of his general socialist philosophy.

He presented that philosophy at the Labour Party Conference in 1949, after Morrison had already begun to speak of the need to consolidate, rather than extend public ownership. His view of the next stage of socialism was:

The kind of society which we envisage, and which we shall have to live in will be a mixed society, a mixed economy, in which all the essential instruments of planning are in the hands of the state, in which the characteristic form of employment will be by the community in one form or another, but where we shall have for a very long time, the light cavalry of private competitive industry.[28]

The speech included a rousing defence of the Labour Government's achievements and a memorable definition of planning:

> What is national planning, but an insistence that human beings shall make ethical choices on a national scale? . . . The language of priorities is the religion of socialism. We have accepted over the last four years that the first claims upon the national product shall be decided nationally, and they have been those of the women, the children and the old people. What is that except using economic planning in order to serve a moral purpose?

In an article in *Tribune* shortly before the 1950 election, Bevan expanded his view of planning and emphasized the great moral task it placed on society:

> The liberal never knew what kind of society he intended until he had, in fact, made it. If we, on the other hand, accept the obligation of planning the direction of economic activity, then we accept with it the burden of deciding who and what must first be served . . . This is the complex answer to those who think socialism is merely a matter of appetite. On the contrary, it is the first time in human history that mankind will have accepted the obligation of free collective moral choice as the ultimate arbiter in social affairs. This, in truth, is the People's Coming of Age.[29]

Immediately after the election, Bevan, with the help of Morgan Phillips and Sam Watson, crushed an attempt by Morrison to establish a new programme which excluded public ownership and which, in the words of Michael Foot, attempted to 'redefine socialism with the rousing tautology': 'socialism means the assertion of social responsibility for matters which are properly of social concern.'[30]

Bevan's victory was short-lived. In April 1951, he re-signed over health charges. In his resignation speech he provided what Michael Foot has called 'the essential epitaph for the whole epoch of Labour Government': 'Take economic planning away from the Treasury, they know nothing about it.'[31]

In terms of electoral support, planning was associated with the hardships of the war and the immediate post-war years. This association was partly the fault of the government itself. The role of planning was essentially negative; it was used to prevent inflation, it was used to prevent the rich getting more than their fair share of resources, it was used to prevent capital resources going to those who were prepared to pay the highest prices for them, and finally, it was used to ensure that resources were used for the production of 'necessities' rather than 'luxuries'. All this was accepted as fair and necessary during the war and the transitional period afterward, but once the extreme shortages of raw materials ended, the negative approach and the instruments associated with it were irrelevant. Harold Wilson could light his 'bonfire of controls' on Guy Fawkes Day 1948 because the controls served no purpose. The government was unable to convince the electorate that planning had a positive role. The critical writings by F. A. Hayek and others[32] launched a fundamental attack on government intervention in the economy and called for the restoration of markets. As a defence of free markets this was unsuccessful; as an attack on socialist planning it was unnecessary. Planning had become an electoral liability; the Conservatives could promise an apparent advance in policy just by promising to abandon it.

Chapter 5: Conservative Planning, 1961–4

The Conservatives announced in 1961 that they were going to introduce planning. ('I am not frightened of the word,' said Selwyn Lloyd.) They established the National Economic Development Office and Council, and it duly produced a five-year economic plan. Some commentators saw this as a sudden and uncharacteristic act. Trevor Smith, for example, speaks of the 'dramatic and almost overnight conversion announced by the Chancellor of the Exchequer on 26 July 1961', and 'the sudden "Damascus Road" conversion of the Conservatives to planning in 1961 . . .'[1] However the idea of planning was by no means alien to the tradition of the Conservative Party and the timing was propitious for a new initiative in economic policy.

The leader of the Conservative Party in 1961 was Harold Macmillan, who had been a strong supporter of planning before the war and who would take a peculiar pleasure in stealing the Labour Party's clothes. In the Cabinet's discussions of Selwyn Lloyd's proposals to introduce planning and to establish the NEDC, Macmillan noted '. . . a rather interesting and quite deep divergence of view between Ministers, really corresponding to whether they had old Whig, Liberal, laissez-faire traditions, or Tory opinions, paternalists and not afraid of a little *dirigisme.*'[2] There was no doubt where Macmillan's sympathies lay: as he said in another context, he felt that 'some degree of state interference – or *dirigisme* – was both necessary and in conformity with traditional Tory philosophy.'[3]

A NEW APPROACH TO ECONOMIC POLICY

The failure of the policies which had seemed to operate so successfully in the early 1950s contributed to a new view of the economic order. These policies combined 'Keynesian' methods of demand management with minimal intervention in industry; after the mid-1950s the outcome of such policies was described as 'stop-go'.

If Keynesian demand management had been successfully carried out, 'stop' and 'go' would have only referred to the government's policy instruments. For example, income tax would have been reduced when there were signs that the growth of demand was slackening and then raised when there were signs that it was accelerating. By these means, total output would have been kept on a smooth path. Instead, the growth of output and demand, far from being kept on a steady path by these measures, moved from periods of rapid growth to periods of near standstill. These changes of speed were the result of deliberate government action. Instead of stabilizing the economy, the government seemed determined to de-stabilize it.

This was due to the government's attempt not only to regulate the level of output (and employment), but also to regulate the overall level of prices and the balance of payments. The typical cycle of stop-go started from a point at which unemployment was rising and the balance of payments was improving. In response to these signs, the government would expand demand which would lead in due course to a rapid increase in imports – to meet the demand – with a resulting deterioration in the balance of payments. At the same time there would probably be signs of accelerating inflation at home. In response to these signs the government would damp down demand. In effect, far from trying to achieve a steady path of output, the government was using its power to alter the path of output to achieve a satisfactory balance of payments and sufficient control of inflation.

Not only did these policies lead to a jerky path of output, they also failed to cure either inflation or the balance of payments problem, both of which showed an underlying tendency to deteriorate.

One possible explanation was that the general approach of Keynesian demand management was correct but that the government was making technical errors in its application. It was suggested that the government mistimed its adjustments to economic policy. It damped down demand just as the economy was moving into recession of its own accord, and expanded the economy just as it was recovering spontaneously. The explanation given for these errors was that either through ignorance or through political cowardice it reacted to the wrong signals. The most sensitive political indicators are unemployment and the current account of the balance of payments. The government expanded demand when the level of unemployment rose, and contracted demand when the balance of payments deteriorated. But there is considerable delay between changes in output and changes in both these indicators.

Today's change in unemployment results from changes in output which happened, on average, six months or more ago. The peak of unemployment is thus likely to be recorded six months or more after the economy has passed the trough of the cycle; that is six months after output has started to recover. Since unemployment figures are reported very rapidly and output figures are reported with some delay, the government tends, so the argument goes, to react at the wrong time. By a similar argument it reacts at the wrong time to balance of payments figures (which are also published very promptly).

Such technical errors would hardly necessitate a major shift in economic policy, but the belief that they were occurring explains part of the general dissatisfaction with current methods of demand management and made it easier for a new approach to be accepted, particularly if it shifted the focus of policy away from the very short term.

The more important question was, why were the problems of inflation and the balance of payments becoming more severe? Added to this was concern with a new objective of policy, economic growth. As far as the balance of payments was concerned, one view voiced strongly by academics and journalists was that the balance of payments problem arose because the government insisted on holding the $2.80 exchange rate and that output was being sacrificed needlessly to a misplaced notion of national pride. The government rejected devaluation as a solution to the problem of the balance of payments; instead it tried to attack what it thought to be the cause, excessive wage increases.

The traditional post-war approach to inflation was to try to regulate it by overall management of the pressure of demand. Relatively speaking this was a liberal policy, since it did not involve direct interference in wage-fixing. It was believed that rapid increases in wages were linked to low levels of unemployment. Empirical basis for this was provided by the 'Phillips curve', called after the late A. W. Phillips, a distinguished economist with an engineering background who first presented his results in a series of lectures at the London School of Economics in 1959. One conclusion drawn from his work was that wage inflation could be reduced or even avoided if unemployment was permanently high enough. This view came to be associated with another economist at the London School of Economics, Frank Paish, who was said to have the ear of the Treasury.

The liberal approach to the control of inflation was thus identified with the Treasury. Part of the new Conservative view was that the Treasury's attitude was wrong and that inflation could be controlled by other means, notably by an incomes policy. (Macmillan's memoirs record his frustration in trying to extract an incomes policy from the Treasury.) Direct control of incomes could thus, it was hoped, solve the problem of both inflation and the balance of payments.

There was a further important development in the economic view, namely the belief that the government could increase the rate of economic growth. Before the late 1950s, economic growth had been an objective of economic policy but had not been given major prominence. When Rab Butler promised in 1954 to double the standard of living in twenty-five years, he was not claiming that this would result from government action, rather that it would result from the Conservative Government's willingness to let private industry get on with it. Growth had not been given major prominence because governments did not believe that they could influence it. The White Paper, *The Economic Implications of Full Employment,* published in

1956, provides a typical example of the government's attitude: 'The Government is pledged to foster conditions in which the nation can, if it so wills, realize its full potentialities for growth in terms of production and living standards.'[4]

'If it so wills' implies at best only modest official support for economic growth. But by 1961 many argued that economic growth was the responsibility of the government and that it should be the prime objective of economic policy.

How was more rapid growth to be achieved? Some held that changes in the approach to demand management would do the trick. Stop-go was particularly blamed for poor growth performance. The technique of running the economy with alternative periods of rapid growth and slow growth was said to make life especially difficult for business. It was argued that manufacturing industry, in particular, could not operate efficiently and plan its investment successfully if the government was erratically expanding and contracting demand. If stop-go could be avoided, investment and innovation would be encouraged and the underlying growth of the economy increased.

A stronger form of this argument suggested that the way to achieve more rapid growth was not simply to discard stop-go but for the government to initiate a period of rapidly increasing demand. This was the policy of the 'dash for growth', which was supposed to shock the economy into a higher rate of investment and hence of sustained growth.

A policy of steady, or still more of rapid growth would presumably entail short-run problems of inflation and the balance of payments. The solution to the problem of inflation was to be an incomes policy. If changes in the exchange rate were ruled out, the economy would, as Dow said, have to 'drive straight through fluctuations in the balance of payments.'[5] But it was not clear that the United Kingdom had sufficient international reserves for such a solution. In the longer term it was hoped that more rapid growth would solve the problems of inflation and the balance of payments.

THE ROLE OF PLANNING

The criticisms of stop-go and proposals for a dash for growth hardly constituted a case for planning. The implied changes in policy, with the important exception of the incomes policy, did not involve new techniques of economic management; they were rather a question of using existing techniques in a new way. It was hoped that one significant change would be the subordination of short-run considerations, such as the balance of payments, to the hoped-for long-run benefits to economic output. That, in a weak sense, was a move to planning.

There was also a new departure in economic management which was claimed to represent a new style of economic planning. This new style was 'indicative planning'. It was presented as a solution to one of the recognized problems of the market economy, that of coordinating decisions about future production and consumption. By contrast with normative planning, under which a central authority tells people what to do, indicative planning is said to relieve problems without threatening democracy.[6]

Indicative planning is a means by which information about the future is exchanged. It can be conducted at various levels of sophistication, but in essence it allows investment decisions to be made with some idea of what future supplies of inputs and demand for outputs will be. It can be particularly valuable in the market for intermediate products, that is, those that are sold to another industry. The steel industry needs to know what coal will be available, the coal industry needs to know how much steel will be produced. The task of coordination can well be carried out by the government. It has a key role as supplier and purchaser in its own right, and it can coordinate decisions without the fear of collusive monopoly that might arise if the task were left to industry.

The role of indicative planning is in principle simply one of coordination. It does not depend on a central plan, and it does not impose compulsion on anyone. It therefore avoids the dangers of bureaucratic intervention: 'It does not require any independent decision-maker to adopt any

85

particular plan; it merely helps him to choose a plan which is more likely to fit in with future market developments.'[7]

At its most modest, indicative planning improves the performance of the economy by avoiding those mistakes which arise through lack of coordination; it does not remove environmental uncertainty but allows the economy to cope with it in a more efficient way. One outcome may be that the amount of investment increases. Before the war it was generally argued that lack of coordination had meant that there was *too much* investment because firms failed to realize that competitors, too, would expand capacity to meet expected increases in demand. But by 1961 it was clear that the supporters of indicative planning hoped that it would increase investment.

Some hoped for more than mere coordination from indicative planning. A Political and Economic Planning study, *Growth in the British Economy*, published in 1960, suggested that one of the reasons for Britain's inadequate growth was that there had never been a growth objective to aim at. 'The desirability of expansion has been alluded to from time to time, but there has never been a clear aim expressed in terms that could enlist the enthusiasm of all sections of the community towards its fulfilment.'[8] The authors argued that publication of a forecast of the possible achievement of the economy for a few years ahead, 'if such an estimate has been carefully drawn up with the cooperation of the people who will be responsible for its realization', might itself make for success. This proposal was precisely the approach adopted first by NEDC and then, in a more extreme form, by the Department of Economic Affairs.

Such an approach goes beyond the question of investment (though investment is a major element) and argues as follows: if you can persuade people that an annual growth rate of, say, four per cent is feasible, they will plan their production on that basis. Provided individual plans are correctly coordinated, through markets and indicative planning, the growth rate will be achieved. The idea is to set a target above past achievement, and then hope that it is achieved through greater confidence.

The model for these claims was the apparent success of planning in France. The PEP study held that under the French system 'the planning of investments was removed from the confusion of current politics, and the desire for economic development was allowed to assert itself.'[9] The French plan is drawn up after a process of consultation between officials, departments and both sides of industry. Once the plan is drawn up, it is obligatory for nationalized industries. There is no compulsion on private industry, but the state has been able to exert pressure initially through the control of raw materials and later through its control of finance.

It has been pointed out, for example by Thomas Wilson,[10] that it was strange that the British followed the French rather than the German example, since the latter's expansion was as remarkable as that of France and was achieved without any use of planning. To the cynic this is unsurprising; to the British middle-class, 'Europe' basically means 'France'. Those who can speak passable French must far outnumber those who can speak German, and British civil servants in particular would admire and somewhat envy their French counterparts. The French approach appealed to their interventionist leanings.

The exchange of visits between the French and British at about this time has often been described. Leruez describes the role of OEEC, PEP, the FBI, the Treasury and the National Institute for Economic and Social Research in these exchanges.

The organization of a three-day conference on Planning in France at Easter 1961, in London, provided clear evidence of the 'complicity' between these various bodies. The initiative for the conference came from a British official at OEEC; it was organized by NIESR; the chief French participants came from the Planning Commissariat, and the conference report appeared in *Planning*, the organ of PEP.[11]

French-style indicative planning was thus to be added to incomes policy and a new approach to demand management in an attempt to solve Britain's recurrent problems of inflation, balance of payments deficits and slow economic growth.

PLANNING AND THE POLITICS OF SUPPORT

A changed view of the economy thus led to a new approach to economic policy which included an element of planning; but how was this change in policy greeted by the electorate?

The Conservative electoral successes of 1955 and 1959 were seen as a vindication of their management of the economy (the electoral slogan of 1955 was 'Invest in Success'), and as a rejection of socialist solutions. In fact the differences between the parties were small and the Conservatives had luck on their side; but Conservative claims to economic know-how involved a price. Economic success had to continue, and the Conservatives had to show that they were not using socialist solutions. This presented a harsh dilemma. Continued economic success required a change in policies; but the proposed solutions to the new problem looked uncomfortably like socialism.

In terms of electoral support there were two important groups. The first was the traditional middle class – small businessmen, managers of established industries and members of the professions. They felt threatened by inflation (though many possessed the ideal investment in the form of a house), and were angry that the government had been so slow to stamp out all traces of socialism. The second group was the new class of managers, executives and administrators in the new industries and professions. They might be upwardly mobile and unwilling to identify themselves with a traditional class. For this group the heat had been taken out of party politics; they were prepared to accept that politics was not a matter of reconciling conflicting interests but of finding technical solutions to problems, particularly those of the economy.

Macmillan's tired cliché of the national cake (the socialists tried to cut equal slices whereas the Conservatives tried to make it bigger) appealed directly to them. They could not understand all the fuss about class conflict, since the obvious solution was to provide more goods for everyone. They were living examples of the end of ideology; they were interested not in political slogans but in economic growth.

This section of the electorate had its counterpart in parliament. There was a new group of politicians in the Conservative Party who did not represent the traditional Conservative interests of land, industry or finance. They were professionals; they could be disparagingly described as career politicians. They included such men as Iain Macleod, Reginald Maudling and Enoch Powell, all of whom entered parliament from the party bureaucracy. They too saw politics as essentially an administrative process.

For these politicians and for the new middle class, 'One Nation' was a natural slogan. As far as economic policy was concerned, it encompassed liberalism and corporatism. The claim of liberal economics is, after all, that the market is a neutral institution, where every penny of demand is of equal value – even if some have more pence than others. In this context the cherished liberal value was 'opportunity,' particularly opportunity for individual advance through energy and ability. Such a view was totally opposed to the Tory belief in traditional class roles. But in the organization of economic activity, central guidance by the intelligent could be preferred to reliance on the market.

This mixture of ideas was typified by the work of the Bow Group: 'The aim of "Setting People Free" has probably been followed as far as, if not further than, is possible in many fields of policy. In other directions the pursuit of "freedom" should certainly mean an extension of the role of the state.' It was prepared to tolerate extensions of public expenditure and it was prepared to espouse planning. 'In the field of economic planning the question is not "has the state a role?" but "What kind of a role must it play?" . . . In a complex industrial society the Government is in fact deeply involved in the business of making Capitalism work.'[12]

Historically the Bow Group was descended from the *Industrial Charter* which had been prepared under Butler's chairmanship, with Macmillan and Stanley among the authors, as a response to the crushing electoral defeat of 1945. Published in 1947, it had aimed to dissociate the party from an identity with policies of laissez-faire and hostility to the Welfare State. As Rab Butler said:

> The *Charter* was, therefore, first and foremost an assurance that, in the interests of efficiency, full employment and social security, modern Conservatism would maintain strong central guidance over the operation of the economy.[13]

The *Charter* intended to provide an alternative to socialism by combining central guidance and individual initiative: 'We point to a way of life designed to free private endeavour from the taunt of selfishness or self-interest and public control from the reproach of meddlesome interference.' It made a clear call for planning: 'There must be strong central guidance . . . Our main economic strategy as a nation needs to be worked out far more surely than it has hitherto.'[14]

The adoption of the *Industrial Charter* was nevertheless followed by a move towards neo-liberalism, but the *Charter* itself was never repudiated, and represented a full statement of the *Étatiste*-corporatist position which was revived by the Bow Group and its parliamentary supporters in the One Nation group.

There were thus two electoral groups to be wooed. The support of the traditional middle class had to be retained and that of the new middle class had to be gained. The election manifesto of 1959, *The Next Five Years*, shows how the task was attempted. There were standard attacks on socialism: 'The socialists have learnt nothing in their period of Opposition save ways to gloss over their true intentions. Their policies are old-fashioned and have no relevance to the problems of the modern world.' And there were appeals to materialism: 'We have shown that Conservative freedom works. Life *is* better with the Conservatives.' But the manifesto was silent on inflation. It made promises on technical advance and adopted a familiar slogan: 'By raising living standards and by social reform we are succeeding in creating One Nation at home.'

The appeal was successful and the Conservatives were given a third term of office; but actions were needed as well as words. A combination of an incomes policy to reassure those alarmed by inflation and a new style of planning for those who sought increased economic growth seemed perfectly designed for the politics of support.

CONSERVATIVE PLANNING IN PRACTICE

Selwyn Lloyd's adoption of planning has been seen as 'a last despairing effort by the Chancellor to show that the government did have a long-term strategy, despite the note of panic in the measures he was announcing.'[15]

The timing may have been tactical but the idea was not revolutionary. Residual fears could be removed by showing that Conservative planning was very different from the despised Labour planning which had been abandoned by 1951. Also the government would need at least the consent if not the active support of industry and the trade union movement if planning was to work.

The announcement was made in Selwyn Lloyd's speech on 25 July 1961 presenting new measures to remedy yet another sterling crisis. He said:

> I will deal first with growth in the economy. The controversial matter of planning at once arises. I am not frightened of the word . . . I think the time has come for a better coordination of these various activities. I intend to discuss urgently with both sides of industry, procedures for pulling together these various processes of consultation and forecasting with a view to better coordination of ideas and plans.[16]

Conservative planning was to differ from socialist planning. It was linked to economic growth rather than to post-war austerity and harmless words like 'consultation', 'forecasting' and 'coordination' were used to allay any fears that this was to be an exercise in central control.

On the following day Selwyn Lloyd expanded his ideas.

> I envisage a joint examination of the economic prospects of the country, stretching five or more years into the future. It would cover the growth of national production and distribution of our resources between the main uses, consumption, Government expenditure, investment, and so on. Above all, it would try to establish what are the essential conditions for realizing potential growth . . .
> . . . That covers, first, the supply of labour and capital, secondly, the balance of payments conditions and the development of imports and exports, and thirdly, the growth of incomes. In other words, I want both sides of industry to share with the Government the task of relating plans to the resources likely to be available.[17]

The claims at this stage were rather modest. 'Realizing potential growth', if it means anything at all, hardly looks like a promise of faster growth. Pressed to reveal more details of the proposed organization, Selwyn Lloyd was deliberately vague, but did promise that it would not simply be a matter of establishing some planning board within the Treasury.

Further details of his ideas were set out in a letter to the TUC and the employers' organizations on 23 September 1961.

> I believe that the time has come to establish a new and more effective machinery for the coordination of plans and forecasts for the main sectors of our economy. There is a need to study centrally the plans and prospects of our main industries, to correlate them with each other and with the government's plans for the public sector, and to see how in aggregate they con-

tribute to, and fit in with, the prospects for the economy as a whole, including the vital external balance of payments. The task of keeping claims on our resources within our capacity is the responsibility of the government. But experience has shown the need for a closer link between government and industry, in order to create a climate favourable to expansion, and make possible effective action to correct weaknesses in our economic structure. This new machinery should, therefore, assist in the promotion of more rapid and sustained economic growth.

The tone is now considerably more optimistic. The 'vital' external balance of payments must be dealt with somehow, but the Chancellor is now talking of a 'climate favourable to expansion'. It is unclear whether this is a matter of faith or whether something will be done in advance to create it. It is also not clear whether the weaknesses in the economic structure are specifically related to growth, or also provide part of the problem of the balance of payments.

The letter also seemed to promise that the new institution would participate actively with the government in all stages of the planning process.

I hope they would . . . obtain a picture, more continuous and comprehensive than has hitherto been available, of the long-term problems in the development of our economy; and this should enhance the value of their advice on, and efforts in, the search for solutions. They would also have better opportunities to help in the moulding of the economic policies at the formative stage.

Selwyn Lloyd also set out the proposals for the National Economic Development Council and Office. The Council would have a membership of about twenty, drawn from government, employers and unions, with the Chancellor of the Exchequer as chairman. The Office 'would not be part of the ordinary government machine'. It would be responsible for the studies of industrial and departmental plans described earlier.

The employers' response to the invitation was fairly predictable. Nigel Harris attributes the main initiative to them; '. . . it was not primarily the Government which promoted the innovation but rather industry, which forced the Government to offer some policy which would avoid fluctuating investment rates.'[18]

The most cited evidence for industry's role in encouraging the government to adopt planning was the FBI conference on *The Next Five Years* held at Brighton in 1960. An account of the conference is given in Sam Brittan's *Steering the Economy*.[19] In contrast to the orthodox view that correcting the balance of payments was the first priority, the conference agreed that an improved rate of growth was the first objective, and that this should help solve the balance-of-payments problem. The conference further accepted the need for some kind of planning to achieve more rapid growth. The immediate cause of this call for planning was a particularly ill-timed intervention in the motor industry where the government had cut home demand just as a world-wide fall in sales was developing. It was an attack on the Treasury's short-term demand management as much as a positive call for planning.

In his account of the FBI, S. Blank[20] saw the 'Brighton revolution' as an important influence on the government's decision to introduce planning and as a sign of a marked change in the role and significance of the FBI. He also suggested that there was a change in public attitudes to businessmen, and that popular mistrust was replaced by a recognition of the importance of managerial skills. W. Grant and D. Marsh[21] question this assertion and the evidence for it. It seems more likely that the employers, partly represented by the FBI, shared the general dissatisfaction with stop-go and were prepared to participate in a new approach to policy, particularly if it promised a more stable environment for investment and hope of government help in controlling wages. There may also have been some shift in opinion in favour of industrial management which made it possible for the Conservative

Government to consult openly with them without raising the cry that it was a capitalist conspiracy. The employers had nothing to lose, and might gain something from joining an experiment in planning.

The TUC was in a much more difficult position. It was being invited to take part in a joint attempt to plan the economy and to improve the growth of output. It might be a golden opportunity but it was very risky. The TUC was not organized to play an active role in the overall management of the economy; a serious attempt to coordinate the views of its members on details of economic policy would require a complete reorganization of its structure. It courted danger if it became openly associated with the government's economic policy. Its traditional role was defensive. As Lord Feather remarked in an interview, the trade union movement 'does not act, it reacts'. It has successfully combined its traditional concern with pay and working conditions with direct access to the government; an open partnership with the government and employers and therefore a shared responsibility for government policies represented a drastic change in its approach. It strongly opposed the pay pause and feared (rightly as it turned out) that there were worse things to come. A serious venture in planning raised again, as it had in the post-war Labour Government, the question of free collective bargaining.

The TUC could not oppose planning in principle. In its report of 1961 it had attacked the government's concern 'with negative and restrictive short-term expedients and a determination to seek a temporary solution to the nation's economic problems at the expense of working people'. It would have to welcome attempts to plan the economy, though left-wing members argued, as before the war, that they had no reason to cooperate with Conservative planning.

The TUC were slow to accept Selwyn Lloyd's invitation. They were in favour of an independent NEDC. They insisted that TUC members should be regarded as representatives of their unions with freedom to report back to them. They were opposed to having 'independents' on the

Council. Finally they demanded that wages policy should be excluded from the NEDC terms of reference. Having been satisfied on their major demands they agreed to join.

At the first meeting of NEDC, held in March 1962, its tasks were defined by the Chancellor of the Exchequer as follows:

(a) To examine the economic performance of the nation, with particular concern for plans for the future in both the private and public sectors of industry.

(b) To consider together what are the obstacles to quicker growth, what can be done to improve efficiency, and whether the best use is made of our resources.

(c) To seek agreement upon ways of improving economic performance, competitive power and efficiency, in other words, to increase the rate of sound growth.

Selwyn Lloyd emphasized that he wanted NEDC to 'have an important impact on government policy during the formative stage, and upon the economic life of the nation.'

NEDC IN ACTION

The authors of the PEP study, *Growth in the British Economy*, regretted that there was no department or minister who could consistently argue the case for economic growth in any discussion of policy: 'If Britain had had a M. Monnet to complain whenever any policy appeared to be adverse to the expansion of production, the rate of growth might have been somewhat faster than it has been.'[22]

The Treasury was always there to argue the case for sterling, the Department of Employment or its predecessor the Ministry of Labour could argue the case for full employment, other departments could argue for their industries or for their spending plans. It was hoped that NEDC would provide the collective voice for economic growth. Since the Office was not part of the government machinery, much would depend on the government's good faith in keeping its promise of full consultation with the Council, and there would then be the much more important question of whether the consultation would influence policy. Since the Treasury retained full responsibility for economic management, relationships between NEDC and the Treasury would be the key issue.

Selwyn Lloyd was sacked by Macmillan in July 1962. His last budget in April 1962 was produced before NEDC had held its second meeting; there had thus been no possible opportunity for consultation. His successor, Reginald Maudling, who had originally been hostile to the founding of NEDC was, however, in favour of an expansionist approach to demand management. His views thus coincided with those who hoped to see an end to the restrictive stop-go policies of the late 1950s. At its second meeting, in May 1962, the Council decided that its main task should be the preparation of a report which studied the implications of a growth rate of four per cent a year between 1961 and 1966. The Office was to carry out an inquiry in the public and private sectors to see what impact such a growth rate would have on them. The Office should also study the implications for manpower, investment and the balance of payments.

The four-per-cent figure was originally intended to be merely hypothetical. It was believed to be large enough to reveal the problems that would have to be solved if faster growth were to be achieved, without being so unrealistic that no one would take the industrial inquiry seriously. However, it rapidly became a target which was accepted by the government, particularly by Maudling. The acceptance of the four-per-cent growth target has been seen as NEDC's greatest achievement, although it seems unlikely that it would have succeeded had not political conditions been right. In particular, as Leruez has argued, it allowed Maudling to take a stronger line against the Treasury. (Though it must not be assumed that the Treasury were opposed to expansion.)

The first NEDC report, *Growth of the United Kingdom Economy to 1966*, was published in February 1963. When it appeared, the economy was in recession, the British application for membership of the Common Market had just

P.E. .—E

been vetoed, and the winter was exceptionally severe. In such circumstances, the growth programme offered hopes of a brighter future, and it was well received. The NEDC report was in two parts; the first part described the results of the industrial inquiry, the second part examined the implications for the economy of four-per-cent growth.

The first part of the report presented the general conclusions of the inquiry into seventeen industries; it covered about two-fifths of the whole national product, and nearly half of industrial production. Detailed results were presented in the annex to the report. The report also tried to provide a general picture of the rest of output. The speed with which the exercise was completed, and its incomplete coverage of industry, made it extremely difficult to determine whether the individual estimates were consistent with each other and with the overall picture of the economy.

The second part of the report set out to answer the following questions:

Will there be enough manpower to meet the needs of all sectors of the economy? Will there be sufficient exports to pay for the necessary imports? Will there be enough savings to finance the necessary investment? Allowing for the needs of public expenditure and investment, will there be sufficient resources to provide a reasonable increase in consumer expenditure?

The answers were generally favourable. They implied that manpower would be broadly sufficient, labour productivity would increase much more rapidly than in the past, and adequate physical capacity would be available. There should be no overall problem of excess demand, and consumers' expenditure should be able to rise much more rapidly than in the past.

There were a number of qualifications to this, most importantly, the question of exports. Exports would have to grow more rapidly than implied by the industrial inquiry. This would require an improvement in competitiveness, partly to expand demand, and partly to make exports more profitable relative to home sales, but there was no indication of how this would come about; for purposes of calculation, it was assumed to happen. At that time, many commentators believed that the best way to improve competitiveness was by devaluation; but NEDC could not have proposed it. Alternatively, the report seemed to say, incomes policies could be relied upon: 'Any temporary worsening of the balance of payments for these or other reasons should prove manageable, provided the rise in money incomes and prices can be sufficiently restrained. . . .'

The final paragraph of the report recalled the perorations of the Labour Government's *Economic Surveys*:

> To sum up, the achievement of an average rate of growth of four per cent per annum between 1961 and 1966 should not prove impossible. There are undoubtedly difficult problems to be tackled, the solution of which will call for changes in policies, arrangements and attitudes. A vital element will be a determination to succeed on the part of Government, management and the trade unions.

The report was favourably accepted and, more importantly, it appeared that Reginald Maudling, the Chancellor of the Exchequer, was committed to its growth target. In the budget speech of April 1963, he said: 'The purpose of the Budget . . . is to do the Government's part in achieving the rate of growth . . . which we have already accepted in the National Economic Development Council.' As Joan Mitchell says:

> 'Commitment in these terms apparently established NEDC firmly in influence, if not in power. NEDC's calculations and projections were actually accepted as a framework for fiscal policy – as, of course, they have to be if NEDC plans are to be more than mildly interesting pieces of research.[23]

As further support for the NEDC approach, the government published, at the end of the year, its first five-year public expenditure programme, which was consistent with the four-per-cent growth rate.

But from that heady start, the influence of NEDC waned. By 1964, the direction of government policy was changing. The budget was deflationary because balance-of-payments difficulties were looming and by mid-1964 the government faced the prospect of defeat in a general election. Maudling became less friendly to NEDC. As Richard Bailey says, 'Too new and radical to have established any precedence, too remote from the Establishment to have any political influence or power, it was in the months before the 1964 Election reduced to a state of impotence.'[24]

A comparison between the targets set out in the NEDC report and actual achievement do not suggest it was a successful exercise. Between 1961 and 1966, total output rose by 2.9 per cent a year, compared with the NEDC target of 4 per cent. Productivity appeared to grow no faster than in the previous five years. (All estimates of the underlying growth of productivity are subject to a large margin of error.) Manufacturing investment grew by 0.2 per cent a year, compared with the target of 3.3 per cent. Exports grew by 3.6 per cent a year, compared with the target of 5 per cent. It is true that the Labour Government had come to power and NEDC's planning role had been taken over by the Department of Economic Affairs; but even by the end of 1964, it had become clear that the system had severe defects.

A major part of NEDC's role had been seen as the provision of a strong link between government and industry, in order that the government could become more aware of industry's detailed problems, and industry could become more aware of the implications of government policies. Yet the establishment of the Economic Development Councils (the 'Little Neddies' which were intended to achieve these links) proceeded only slowly.

The independence of NEDC from the machinery of government became, in the end, a net disadvantage. The government could ignore it when it chose to do so, and did not feel bound by its proposals. This, in turn, affected NEDC's approach. If the NEDC plan was to be more than simply an indicative plan, if it was to achieve changes in the structure of the economy that required more than a matter of coordination, it had to make some concrete proposals and hope they would influence government policy. However, it lacked the power. Its second report, *Conditions Favourable to Faster Growth*, was designed to show how the four-per-cent growth rate might be achieved. It included some sensible discussion of regional policy and of problems of labour mobility and redundancy; but it was a tentative document, and included, as Leruez says, 'a number of well-meaning but ineffectual platitudes'.

It omitted any discussion of the policy choices that would have to be made, particularly in the short run, if faster growth was to be achieved. It called for some kind of incomes policy. On the sensitive issue of the balance of payments, it said that the prospect of a deficit should not deter the government from pursuing expansion, arguing that the balance of payments would be stronger once a higher rate of growth had been achieved, and meanwhile the government should use all its borrowing resources to see us through the temporary difficulties. That was a popular enough view, but NEDC had no means of imposing it on the government.

The initial success of NEDC occurred because it met a political need. A new policy departure was needed, which NEDC symbolized. The Chancellor of the Exchequer was its chairman, suggesting that its views would be taken seriously. It was separate from the Treasury, so perhaps it would be free of the so-called 'Treasury orthodoxy'. In addition, the emphasis on growth as a long-term objective coincided with Maudling's view that we could break through our problems in a 'dash for growth'. But faced with the greater difficulties associated with the emerging balance of payments deficit, NEDC was ignored. In the discussions of economic policy, there was still no 'minister for economic growth'. The Labour Party was determined to avoid that mistake.

I have argued that the introduction of planning was not an extraordinary act for the Conservative Party, particularly when it was led by an avowed Tory in the person of

Harold Macmillan. One may also ask whether, in the event, there was much of a radical change in policy. From 1963, the government, using conventional demand management, embarked on a dash for growth; it was a more extreme version than usual of the 'go' stage of the cycle. Even before the Conservatives left office, they were moving over to the 'stop' phase. A new institution was founded, an ambitious target was set and three reports were published; but the plan did not impose any constraints on short-run policies. Whether it would have solved the short-run problems if given long enough cannot be known; when those short-run problems became too severe, the government adopted conventional solutions and ignored the plan.

Chapter 6: The Labour Party and the National Plan, 1964–6

The Labour Party was, understandably, taken aback by the Conservative Government's establishment of a planning machinery. It could hardly attack planning: after some hesitation it put itself forward instead as the only party which could exploit fully the benefits of the scientific and technological revolution. It had a number of points in its favour. Harold Wilson, the economist with the formidable memory, seemed a more plausible leader to the promised land of high technology than his two predecessors as Prime Minister – Harold Macmillan, who seemed determined to portray himself as a relic of a more gracious age, and whose government was seriously embarrassed by the Profumo scandal and Sir Alec Douglas Home, 'the fourteenth earl', who epitomized the 'grouse moor' image of the Conservative Party.

The Labour Party stressed the differences between its own concept of planning and that of the Conservatives. Labour planning was to be 'purposive' and 'effective'; it must 'have teeth in it somewhere'. The Labour Party's election manifesto, *Let's Go with Labour for the New Britain*, was bitter: 'A death-bed repentance may ease the Tory conscience, but it is a cynical and utterly unacceptable substitute for the lifelong sincerity and solidarity of the Labour Party on this crucial issue. Tory devices – or Labour planning?' The Conservative claim in *Prosperity with a Purpose* was rather weak. 'All human activity involves planning. The question is: how is the planning to be done? By consent or by compulsion?' The electorate either did not care or doubted that the alternatives were so extreme. The Labour Party was elected, but the changes it made were small compared with the continuity of policy between the Conservative and Labour Governments:

The characteristic themes of the Wilson Government in its first three years of office – whether the emphasis on incomes policy, the regional approach to unemployment, the National Plan, the attempt to join the Common Market, the long-term regulation of Government expenditure, the idea of continuous economic regulation, instead of merely Budgets, or even (in embryonic form) the stress on physical 'supply side' problems had already been adopted by Conservative Ministers very early in the 1960s.'[1]

The similarity to Conservative policies was to be expected from a party which had been unable to develop an alternative approach to economic policy during its years in opposition.

LABOUR AND THE THIRTEEN WASTED YEARS

The central issue in the bitter internal Labour Party disputes of the opposition years had been how far public ownership was necessary for the achievement of the party's objectives. Planning was inevitably linked to that issue. Was planning necessary, and if so, could it be introduced in a mixed economy? Those on the left argued that detailed planning was necessary and could only be achieved if public ownership dominated the economy. Revisionists accepted a rather different style of planning – based mainly on the overall management of the economy – and believed that it could be applied to a mixed economy.

After 1951, the Labour Party had to explain why the Labour Government had abandoned planning. The Bevanites thought it was necessary and had failed because it had been attempted in a mixed economy; the revisionists argued that detailed planning of the type attempted after 1945 was no longer needed.

Revisionism was part of the general 'end of ideology' movement of the 1950s whose effects had also been felt in the Conservative Party. It had a deeper relevance to the Labour Party since it questioned its traditional hostility to capitalism. The debate had begun before the war with such works as *The Modern Corporation and Private*

Property[2] in which A. Berle and G. Means described the waning role of the capitalist entrepreneur and the emergence of the manager of the large corporation. They argued that the power of competitive markets was waning and would have to be replaced by state regulation. Similarly, James Burnham in *The Managerial Revolution*[3] saw the replacement of laissez-faire capitalism by a managerial society ruled by scientists, technologists and the organizers of production. After the war, similar themes were developed by Galbraith, and the 'convergence' of Western and communist societies, particularly in their economic organization, was stressed by writers such as Clark Kerr.[4] The sustained post-war boom in the Western economies also seemed to show that modern capitalism was successful.

The most influential figure to apply these ideas to the Labour Party was Anthony Crosland, particularly in *The Future of Socialism* (1956). His basic argument, which appeared in 'The Transition from Capitalism', was that capitalism had changed its nature and that its abolition was no longer necessary for the achievement of socialist objectives. Capitalism had been replaced by statism. The change represented a major social revolution:

> With its arrival, the most characteristic features of capitalism have all disappeared: the absolute rule of private property, the subjection of the whole of economic life to market influences, the domination of the profit motive, the neutrality of government, the typical laissez-faire division of income, and the ideology of individual rights. This is no minor modification: it is a major historical change.[5]

Once capitalism had been replaced by statism, the old arguments for public ownership and detailed planning were no longer valid. Crosland proposed that controls over industry should be directed to certain basic planning ends: full employment, the balance of payments, the location of industry, etcetera. Beyond this, they should not be multiplied.

Within the framework of overall government planning, the proper way to make the private sector responsive to the needs of the community is to make it competitive. The failure to do so was perhaps the greatest single failure of the post-war Labour administration.[6]

Public ownership was no longer central to party policy but had become at best a doubtful means to an end. The analysis is Keynesian: attend to overall demand management (though at this stage Crosland was still prepared to see direct controls used as an instrument of demand management) and leave the allocation of resources to the market and competition.

The penultimate chapter of *The Future of Socialism* is devoted to the role of planning. Crosland suggested that the debate had lost much of its vigour because the Conservatives now accepted a degree of responsibility for the management of the economy which would have been outrageous to a previous generation. Similarly, socialist views on planning had been modified.

The pre-war argument, based as it was on the combination of manifest inefficiency and glaring inequality, displayed by the capitalism of the 1930s, has in any case lost much of its force in the expansionist full employment economy and the Welfare State of the 1950s.[7]

Crosland argued that the failure of post-war planning had been a political failure.

If socialists want bolder planning, they must simply choose bolder ministers and – just as important – themselves accept a greater degree of self-restraint when the results of planning impinge unpleasantly, as they often will, on their constituents or their own pet spheres of interest.[8]

There was no shortage of planning techniques; what was needed was political will. Provided the correct macroeconomic allocations could be achieved and the problems of inflation avoided, Crosland saw little need for detailed planning within each sector. The traditional socialist case for such planning, based on the divergence between production for profit and for use, was far less applicable now that standards of material welfare were higher.

The onus of proof, argued Crosland, should always be on those who wanted to override the market allocation of resources within the total allocated to a sector. He was unimpressed by the view that the government should frequently intervene because of its 'superior knowledge', particularly of the future. Such intervention would only be justified if the government obviously had a clearer view of future demand than private industry – there was no reason to think this would normally be true in consumption and export markets – and if it were then prepared to enforce intervention in the face of formidable political obstacles.

Crosland's view was that provided the government could succeed in enlarging the industrial base, the remaining ninety per cent of the United Kingdom economy could be left to look after itself. It was against these revisionist arguments that Bevan and the other supporters of public ownership fought so vigorously. In his last speech

at the Labour Party Conference at Blackpool in 1959, Bevan said:

> I believe that it is possible for a modern intelligent community to organize its economic life rationally, with decent orders of priority, and it is not necessary to resort to dictatorship in order to do it. That is why I am a Socialist. . . . Our main case is, and must remain, that in modern complex society, it is impossible to get rational order by leaving things to private economic adventure. . . . We will never be able to get the economic resources of this nation fully exploited unless we have a planned economy in which the nation itself can determine its own priorities.[9]

Despite his eloquence, the Labour Party was not prepared to adopt a programme of extensive public ownership.

But nor was the revisionist case for increased reliance on competitive market forces accepted.

The Future of Socialism was written against a background of the apparent success of 'Butskellite' policies. But in the later 1950s, as those policies began to fail, and as there was greater stress on the need for economic growth, the Labour Party as a whole shifted towards a more interventionist approach to economic policy.

The development of the party's ideas on planning was marked by *Plan for Progress*, produced in 1958 by a sub-committee of the National Executive Committee. Its proposals were similar to Crosland's, though with a stronger attack on the now apparently failing Conservative policies. (1958 was the first year since the war in which total output had actually fallen.)

Plan for Progress considered the choice to be between the present path of short-lived and disastrous dashes for 'freedom', and 'the high road of sustained expansion, planning to achieve higher investment and full employment, along with more stable prices and a strong balance of payments.'[10] Planning did not mean a return to more detailed controls; day-to-day decisions could be left to industry and the consumer. Planning was concerned with the larger decisions – matching savings with investment, imports with exports, spending with production, and jobs with workers. 'The object of planning will be to provide a broad framework within which the creation of new wealth can go smoothly and rapidly ahead, and the detailed decisions of industry do not come into conflict with national objectives.'

That sounds very moderate. It is close to Crosland's proposals and, indeed, it hardly seemed to differ from what the Conservatives were attempting. But there were some new proposals (or rather, a revival of old proposals). For example, planning should be concerned with increasing the production of those types of goods which are needed in the national interest, and 'where necessary holding back those which are less essential'.

There was considerable emphasis on investment. A league table showed that the United Kingdom allocated a smaller proportion of its output to investment than any other European country except Belgium. Investment was seen as the instrument of growth and the main objective of planning was to increase it. The tax system would be used to encourage investment and discourage dividends. There would be controls over companies' internal funds, and large companies would be required to report their short-term and long-term investment plans. If necessary, building controls would be used to direct investment. The pre-war proposal to establish a National Investment Board was revived.

Some of these proposals were incorporated, in a much attenuated form, in the election manifesto of 1959, *Britain Belongs to You*. The manifesto talked of planned expansion, but gave no indication how it was to be achieved. Public ownership was to be extended to steel and road haulage. There were no other plans for future nationalization, but where an industry is shown 'after thorough inquiry' to be failing the nation, it could be taken into public ownership if necessary.

In 1963, the Labour Party published *Signposts for the Sixties*. It appeared after Selwyn Lloyd's announcement of Conservative planning but made no reference to it. In retrospect one is struck by its combination of vague optimism with vaguer proposals; but at the time it made a serious counter-appeal to those being wooed by Conservative promises of unity and progress. It began, 'We live in a scientific revolution.' Its solution to British complacency and its method for halting 'piecemeal economic deterioration and gradual political decline' was a plan for economic growth. 'A national plan, with targets for individual industries – especially the key sectors which produce the tools for expansion – would enable every industry and undertaking, publicly or privately owned, to plan its own development with confidence in the future.'

There would be a National Industrial Planning Board, integrated with the government's own planning machinery and in close touch with both sides of industry. Its main task would be to 'ensure speedy and purposive industrial investment'. It would be helped by tax and financial policies, and there would be greater control over pension funds and private insurance companies. In support of the national plan, public ownership would be used to acquire a stake in the growth points of the British economy, to control industries which relied on government assistance, and to counter-balance the concentrations of economic power in the giant corporations.

This went much further than Selwyn Lloyd's proposals, particularly in the emphasis on public ownership, but inevitably it looked less as if the Labour Party was climbing on to the bandwagon than as if it were trying desperately to pretend that it had never climbed off. It was the Conservatives who took the initiative of reintroducing planning; the Labour Party was still afraid of its associations with die-hard socialism or post-war austerity.

The Conservatives recognized that the growing interest in economic growth and the apparent failure of Keynesian policies to achieve it called for a new approach to economic policy, and they were prepared to adopt planning. They caught the Labour Party without a constructive approach of its own, and it had hurriedly to show that it was the natural party to organize planning, and had important ideas of its own.

THE DEPARTMENT OF ECONOMIC AFFAIRS
AND THE NATIONAL PLAN

One of the first acts of the new Labour Government in 1964 was to establish the Department of Economic Affairs. According to Harold Wilson, 'This new department would be concerned with real resources, with economic planning, with strengthening our ability to export and to save imports, with increasing productivity, and our competitiveness in domestic markets.'[11] It appeared that Bevan's final advice, 'Take economic planning away from the Treasury', had been adopted. (George Brown, who headed the new department, had, ironically, been one of Bevan's strongest opponents.)

There was debate about the respective roles of the

Treasury and the DEA. An official proposal that there should be a distinction between short-term responsibilities (the Treasury) and long-term planning (the DEA) was rejected. Wilson, Brown and Callaghan produced a concordat which

> . . . made clear the fundamental distinction between monetary responsibilities on the one hand, which must come under the Treasury, and, on the other, the coordinating responsibilities for industry and everything to do with the mobilization of real resources for productivity and exports.[12]

George Brown thought that the setting up of the DEA 'envisaged a wholly novel form of national social accountancy to replace the financial accountancy by which the Treasury has always dominated British life.'[13] We shall consider in due course whether this distinction is either meaningful or useful; but it illustrated the Labour Government's hope that it was inaugurating a new era of economic policy, freed from the restraints which it attributed to the 'Treasury view'.

The DEA acquired many of NEDC's economists and industrial experts; it also acquired some economists from the Treasury and the Regional Development Division from the Board of Trade. Its first task was to produce a plan. The balance of payments crisis of late 1964, coupled with the government's determination to preserve the value of the pound, meant that the NEDC plan was already in jeopardy; it was replaced by a target growth of 25 per cent between 1964 and 1970 (about 3.8 per cent a year, compared with NEDC's target of 4 per cent a year from 1961 to 1966). It was produced in the amazingly brief time of eleven months and presented in September 1965.

The National Plan, in R. Bailey's words, was 'a mixture of forecast, feasibility study, policy directive, industrial targetry and a dissertation on the economic facts of life'.[14] In the foreword, George Brown said:

> The publication by the Government of a plan covering

all aspects of the country's economic development for the next five years is a major advance in economic policy-making in the United Kingdom. Prepared in the fullest consultation with industry, the plan for the first time represents a statement of government policy, and a commitment to action by the government.[15]

He emphasised that the most serious problem was the balance of payments. The deficit had to be eliminated and past debts had to be repaid. This meant that export performance had to improve, which required greater competitiveness and efficiency. 'The plan sets out the policies and the actions needed to achieve these ends.' The achievement of 25-per-cent growth would require planning of investment, manning and training. 'If industry is to do this, it must have a clear picture of the potential growth of the economy four or five years ahead: this the plan provides.'

The government was totally committed to the growth target; failure would be seen as a failure of government policy. Two different types of planning were involved. The balance of payments weakness was a structural problem, which would require specific 'policies and actions', implying that the government was going to adopt a positive planning role, and, presumably, believed that it had adequate instruments to achieve its objectives. As far as the growth of output was concerned, what firms needed was a 'clear picture of the potential growth of the economy . . .'. In other words, the hope was that indicative planning would raise the rate of growth of output.

The plan's disquisition on the nature and purpose of planning began by saying that although the British economy was mixed, the government had great economic power and influence. 'They intend to use this to secure faster growth and national solvency.' Most of industry and commerce was governed by the market economy, 'But this does not necessarily, and without active government influence, bring about the results which the nation needs – for example, sufficient exports to pay for our imports and other overseas expenditure.'

An exercise in indicative planning alone would not achieve the required structural shift towards exports. But the positive planning proposals offered were partial or tentative. The plan included a 'Check-list of Action Required'. Under the heading 'The Balance of Payments', the following actions were listed:

Defence expenditure will be reduced.

Aid to developing countries will be restrained and the effectiveness of each pound of aid increased.

Private investment abroad will be limited.

There will be a major development of 14 ports.

Plans will be made for speeding up export traffic.

Studies will be made, industry by industry, of ways of increasing exports.

Government, British National Export Council and other organizations will assist exporters.

Plans will be made, industry by industry, to save imports.

There will be a selective programme of agricultural expansion.

The policy for productivity, prices and incomes will be pursued.

A sceptic would be unconvinced that a new approach had been found for solving the balance-of-payments problem.

The problem of the balance of payments was the clearest case in which indicative planning was unlikely to achieve the desired result. The calculations made for the plan revealed another. When all the sums had been done, there was a 'manpower gap' of 400,000 men. In other words, the forecast demand for labour exceeded the fourcast supply of labour by that number. This was a substantial number in relation to the expected increase in labour supply. The 'Check-list of Action Required' to solve this problem was unimpressive.

As an exercise in indicative planning, *The National Plan* included a rather more elaborate exercise than that of the NEDC plan. The general approach was the same; an industrial inquiry was made, covering all industries, rather than just two-thirds. The responsibility for completion of the questionnaire lay with the EDCs, but they only covered a small part of industry; most of the inquiry was carried out by NEDO or by the sponsoring departments. Since the coverage was nearly complete, it was possible to check the internal consistency of the answers. One could examine whether the total added up to a growth of 25 per cent over the period, and whether estimates of supply of each commodity matched estimates of demand. It is quite unlikely that they would at the first attempt. A process of 'iteration' is required until plans are consistent. Further, they need to be consistent with the expected pattern of final demand. The rushed procedure meant that there was little time for this process. Where inconsistencies remained, they should have provided a useful guide to potential supply problems, but, as Bailey remarks, 'Reading . . . the so-called Industry Annexes, it is unusual to come across anything which throws light on the problems or prospects of the industries reported on'.[16]

The industrial inquiry was not a particularly valuable exercise. Industry was sceptical about the growth target, and did not have to take the questionnaire seriously. There was a problem of coordinating industry replies. Many firms do not plan five years ahead, and would be unlikely to devote much effort to a hypothetical exercise. To quote Bailey again: 'Looking at the forecasts in retrospect, it would be interesting to know how many companies felt that they were less in the dark, as a result of reading the Industrial Annex covering their particular activities, than they were before.'[17]

THE END OF THE NATIONAL PLAN

R. G. Opie described the National Plan as 'conceived October 1964, born September 1965, died (possibly murdered) July 1966'.[18] In its brief life it had little chance to influence policy, but its growth objectives were being undermined throughout the Labour Government's term of office. The plan was widely noticed on the day of its publication and played some role in the election campaign of 1966 which gave Wilson a comfortable majority. But almost immediately after the election there was a further sterling crisis, which resulted in deflationary policies. Then, 'On 20 July, the demise of the National Plan was announced. It had of course been suspected dead for a long time past.'[19]

There are a number of ways of discussing the National Plan and of attempting to learn from its failure. One approach is to view it narrowly as an exercise in planning and to comment on its lack of adequate instruments. That approach assumes that the exercise was worthwhile in itself, and is concerned only with its effectiveness.[20] Another approach sees the failure in terms of the sacrifice of the objective of economic growth to that of preserving the exchange rate. It has provoked such comments as 'When it came to the point, the maintenance of the exchange rate was preferred to faster growth (or even to any growth at all), and to the maintenance of full employment.'[21] Or, 'Yet again, as under the Conservatives but in even more striking fashion, the defence of the pound was put before expansion.'[22]

Those who made such comments may not have believed in planning, but they certainly believed in economic growth. If growth was being held back because of Britain's poor export performance, the problem, they believed, could be solved by changing the exchange rate; but this was not politically acceptable. As Brittan said in his penetrating criticism of the National Plan, 'Devaluation, which is the standard means of making exports more competitive, or more profitable, and imports more expensive in the home market, had been summarily rejected.'[23]

That view raises a question which applied to both the Conservative and Labour attempts at planning. Was growth held back because undue attention was paid to the balance of payments and the exchange rate? To put the question another way, is there a genuine political choice between growth and a stable exchange rate? To their great discredit, those who took the decision to abandon growth in 1966 probably believed that there was such a choice. As explained in Chapter 2, the experience of devaluation in 1967, and more particularly of flexible exchange rates since 1972, casts severe doubts on this view. The weak exchange rate was a symptom, not a cause of Britain's economic problems.

The Labour Government's attempt at planning raises certain key questions. In particular there is the much discussed question of the establishment of the DEA as a rival institution to the Treasury. Was it possible or sensible to keep the Treasury out of economic planning? (The most extreme gesture was the exclusion of the Chancellor of the Exchequer from NEDC.) If there are conflicts in economic policy, for example between growth and price stability, then it may be sensible to devise separate departments so that the issues can be debated openly in the Cabinet rather than patched up behind one set of doors. Further, if a particular objective is believed to have been wrongly neglected in the past, it may be sensible to appoint an energetic minister to press its case strongly in future. Such changes, however, cannot alter the economic constraints within which the government has to operate. In Andrew Gamble's term, they do not alter the politics of power.[24]

Unfortunately the establishment of the DEA seemed to persuade George Brown, in particular, that the constraints had changed. Hence his distinction between 'national social accountancy' and the Treasury's 'orthodox financial accountancy'. There is surely less in this than meets the eye. It is well recognized that there is a distinction between 'social' and 'private' costs, and as far as possible, the distinction is taken into account in making public expenditure decisions. It is possible that he had in mind a preference for physical rather than financial forms of regulation – that is, that resources were to be allocated by fiat rather than by prices. But that had nothing to do with the Treasury's alleged obsession with financial accounting. Insofar as it has responsibility for economic management, the Treasury has to be aware of the constraints on the economy. In an open economy, if we try to consume more than we produce, the result is likely to be a deterioration in the balance of payments, or a fall in the exchange rate, leading in turn to higher inflation, or both. The constraints are there, however they are measured. The Treasury was made the guardian of the exchange rate, and was therefore bound to warn when problems were imminent.

If the technical constraints were unchanged (and the National Plan was notably short of proposals for changing them) there might always be some hope that policy priorities might be altered. It is here that the history of the plan is most extraordinary.

Lord George-Brown commented on the failure thus:

> One of the assumptions we made was that the plan would take priority and other policies pursued by the Government would be made to fit its provisions. In the event this was not done, as I have shown, and as a result the 4-per-cent growth rate was made impossible of achievement. I still believe that there was not all that much wrong with the plan – it was our failure to adhere to it.[25]

The first sentence is ambiguous. Does it mean that Lord George-Brown believed that the plan and all its implications had been accepted by the Cabinet and they promised *thereafter* that it would take priority? If so, they clearly broke the promise. Or does it mean that while he was constructing the plan, he believed it would take priority? But that would imply an absurdly open-ended commitment by the Cabinet to whatever policies it were to contain. To state such a case is to reject it. The 'assumption' seems to have been a guess; it was not a sensible one. The most alarming thought is that the problems were not discussed at all until it was too late, that Lord George-Brown never went to the Cabinet and pointed out that the growth target was not feasible with a fixed exchange rate and that before the plan was drawn up, they must choose between them.

The last sentence is equally revealing. What could 'failure to adhere' to the plan have meant? There was an output target, certainly, but there was also a balance-of-payments and balance-of-trade target. The plan was quite clear that the balance of payments was a first priority; there was no commitment to pursue economic growth regardless. If there had been a clear set of actions related to the plan's objectives, it would have been possible, after the event, to point to sectors of the economy and blame them for failing to take such actions. Apart from the trivial sense in which one could perhaps have pointed to exporters and said that they did not export enough (why should they have done so?), no such accusing finger could be pointed. This was because there was no such list of actions. There was a set of ambitious forecasts, and a list of feeble policies which would do no harm but did not go nearly far enough towards solving the problems.

Harold Wilson's comment on the experiment is characteristic.

It was a brave effort. It was right. It was the events of 1966 and 1967, which proved that we did not have the time for the Plan to work in real terms – production, exports, import-saving – before short-term speculative factors overwhelmed us. What it did set out to do was fulfilled – but two years later.[26]

Chapter 7: The Aftermath of National Planning

With the death of the National Plan, as Brittan said, 'one particular approach to economic policy had lost its credibility in this country for the rest of this decade, and probably beyond.'[1] After ten years, there has been no attempt to revive national economic planning. There have been a number of official medium-term projections, but their role as plans or as government targets has usually been strenuously denied.

In 1969, the DEA published *The Task Ahead: Economic Assessment to 1972*. (Nobody is ever quite sure what an Assessment is; but it is certainly neither a forecast nor a plan.) It started:

> This is a planning document, not a plan. That is to say, the document provides a basis for a further stage in the continuing process of consultation between Government and both sides of industry about major issues of economic policy.[2]

The document was extremely cautious: '. . . it is highly provisional . . . It is not a blue-print.' It presented a 'wedge' approach to economic prospects, with the range of possible outcomes broadening through time. It laid down three broad objectives: a substantial surplus in the balance of payments, a steady improvement of competitive efficiency and an improvement in regional balance. As with *The National Plan*, there were few positive proposals about how these objectives would be achieved.

Unlike *The National Plan*, *The Task Ahead* did not include detailed industrial studies. The document was intended as the beginning of such a process; consultations were to take place with industry, mainly through the Economic Development Councils. It provided what it called a 'possible pattern of growth' for seven industries. The consultations proposed in *The Task Ahead* were carried out during 1969. In 1970, the Treasury, which had taken over the DEA's role, published *Economic Prospects to 1972 – a Revised Assessment*, which took those consultations into account. The approach was again cautious: 'Like *The Task Ahead*, the revised assessment is not itself a plan, but is put forward as a basis for forward planning and decision-making, both by Government and industry.'[3]

By the end of 1969, the major objective of *The Task Ahead* – a balance of payments surplus – had been achieved. No further shift of resources was required. The *Revised Assessment*, nevertheless, took a generally cautious line. The assumption for the growth of output was that it would be in line with the *past* growth of potential output. No allowance was made for a more rapid growth of productivity, or for greater use of capacity. The policy implications were put mainly in terms of the allocation of resources to consumption, public expenditure, investment and the balance of trade. On investment, it adopted a characteristically sceptical line. 'There is at present no reliable means of forecasting total investment over the medium term, nor of estimating how much investment would be required to support a given increase in productive capacity.' In the end, it concluded that an increase in investment was desirable. It recognized that more resources could now be devoted to domestic spending, but it warned against excessive growth.

It is difficult to believe that either of the documents played a major role in government policy or in industrial decision-making. From 1966 to 1970, the government was more concerned with the short-run problems of first attempting to avoid devaluation, and then trying to make it work.

CONSERVATIVE GOVERNMENT, 1970-4

When the Conservative Government came to power in 1970 it had the evidence, albeit rather negative, from two earlier experiments in economic policy. Previous Conservative Governments had tried Keynesian demand management and found it inadequate. It had failed to prevent inflation and balance of payments problems, or to encourage rapid economic growth. Planning was then tried instead, and Harold Macmillan had presided over an experiment which had been continued by the Labour Government. That too had failed. If neither Keynesian demand management nor planning were successful, what policies could the new government pursue?

The initial impression was that it would move markedly away from interventionism toward the party's old liberal economic traditions. Part of the evidence was provided by reported sightings of 'Selsdon Man', named after the Selsdon Park Hotel where the conference was held to draft the party's election manifesto. It appears that he was a *canard*, based on a one-sided view of the conference's conclusions. The manifesto was not notably radical, though it did emphasize a more liberal line:

> . . . we reject the detailed intervention of socialism, which usurps the function of management, and seeks to dictate prices and earnings in industry. We much prefer a system of general pressures, creating an economic climate which favours and rewards enterprise and efficiency. Our aim is to identify and remove obstacles that prevent effective competition and restrict initiative.[4]

The early actions of the Heath administration seemed consistent with this approach. The National Incomes Commission and the Prices and Incomes Board were abolished, as was the Consumers' Council. NEDO seemed threatened, and planning became a taboo word in Whitehall. (It is said that one official was not allowed to attend a meeting of European planners until its title was changed to the Group on Medium-Term Assessments.) Industrial lame ducks – Tony Benn had been the originator of the expression – were not to be spared.

Yet from these early claims of economic liberalism (Heath had, after all, fought a hard battle for the abolition of resale price maintenance) the Conservatives moved closer to corporatism than any previous government, with its pursuit of administrative and collective solutions to economic problems rather than reliance on markets. In the end, it was a form of corporatism which excluded the trade unions, who were confronted first by the government's industrial relations policy and then by its strenuous defence of its incomes policy. The government's general economic policy can be described as the apotheosis of crude Keynesianism. It was tested to the point of destruction, and was destroyed. It was a remarkable experience, and merits study because the lessons from it set new limits for ideas of what economic policy can achieve, and in retrospect, cast new light on the policy failures of the 1960s and on the downfall of the National Plan. At the end of the experiment, the UK experienced within a relatively short period during 1974 and 1975 the most rapid rate of inflation, the largest balance-of-payments deficit, and the highest level of unemployment since the war. It also saw the most severe and prolonged fall in the value of shares. (Inflation and the balance of payments improved subsequently, while unemployment continued to rise.)

The Conservative Government's policies can be explained as the application of a highly simplified version of Keynes's ideas. It used an analysis developed for conditions of high unemployment to one in which there was near full employment, and it completely ignored Keynes's views on inflation and on the role of the money supply in generating inflation.

The key to their policies was the rapid increase in unemployment during 1971 which was accompanied by accelerating inflation. The earlier belief that inflation could be prevented by high unemployment began to be eroded. Explanations for the breakdown of the so-called 'Phillips curve' varied from the collapse of moral standards to the arrival of left-wingers at the head of major trade unions. The important conclusion for demand management was that if high unemployment no longer prevented inflation, we could perhaps solve the two problems simultaneously. Unemployment could be reduced by the conventional methods of demand management, and inflation could be controlled by some other means. Incomes policy was the chosen method for the latter. A similar technique had been used in the 1960s planning experiments, but then it was generally recognized that attempts to increase output rapidly would put strain on incomes policies. In 1972 it was believed that the reverse might be true, and that rapid expansion of demand might actually help slow down inflation. Thus, in spite of an alarming rate of inflation – by the standards of those days – there was an expansionary budget in 1972 followed by further expansion in 1973. Incomes policies were introduced in 1972. Meanwhile, partly as a result of new methods of controlling the monetary system and partly as a result of fiscal policy, the money supply started to increase rapidly during 1971 and 1972. The possibility that the result would be increased inflation was not taken too seriously.

Along with a combined incomes policy and fiscal and monetary expansion there was a move (in June 1972) from fixed exchange rates to flexible rates. The introduction of 'threshold' wage payments system in the autumn of 1973, shortly before the quadrupling of oil prices and a general explosion of commodity prices, produced the further twist in the inflationary spiral which eventually sent inflation to a twelve-month rate of twenty-seven per cent.

The chief characteristic of this period was the attempt to over-ride or deny the existence of market forces. Inflation, in particular, became something that could be negotiated away. Part of the bargain consisted of promises of increases in real wages, as if these, too, were in the government's gift. When negotiation failed, the government resorted to confrontation. In so doing, as Gamble has argued, Heath abandoned the Conservative tradition of One Nation, and the electorate voted for the more conciliatory attitudes of a Labour Government.

FROM ECONOMIC PLANNING TO INDUSTRIAL STRATEGY

The Labour Government's current Industrial Strategy is

the most recent version of economic planning. It is planning of a very modest type, and given the government's concentration on major short-term problems its main role so far has been as part of the promise of a better tomorrow when today's problems are over. It is also presented, though without much conviction, as the Labour Government's way of avoiding such short-term problems in the future.

The Industrial Strategy is a dilution of proposals that originated from the left wing of the Labour Party. The progression of these ideas from left-wing theory to Government policy is unusually well documented. The theory is presented in Stuart Holland's *The Socialist Challenge*.[5] Before considering its arguments we must set it in the context of post-war Labour Party thought.

I have argued that the main setback to the Labour Party's pre-war commitment to public ownership and planning was Keynes's view that overall demand management was an adequate substitute and could solve the problem of unemployment. Keynesianism seemed to work; full employment was achieved after the war, and the Labour Party was able to achieve many of its major social aims by the development of the Welfare State within the mixed economy. Continuing attacks on capitalism could not therefore rely on its tendency to produce high and prolonged levels of unemployment, nor could they rely on its tendency to produce widespread poverty and suffering. The attacks had therefore to be fundamental. Capitalism was rejected as a moral system. The revisionists, notably Anthony Crosland, not only accepted the Keynesian approach but also argued that capitalism had so changed its nature that the fundamentalist attacks on its moral basis were mistaken. The revisionists accepted but did not stress planning, and favoured the use of markets and competition.

Neither the revisionists nor the fundamentalists captured the party, and the uneasy compromise that resulted stressed ends rather than means and left the Labour Party without a clear approach to economic policy. Holland's contribution offered a chance to escape from the dilemma whereby fundamentalism is electorally too extreme to be popular, while revisionism can be so close to moderate conservatism that the electorate may believe its policies best run by the Conservatives. Holland offers a non-fundamentalist attack on capitalism. Once again, the problem with capitalism became not that it is immoral but that it is inefficient. There were new arguments for public ownership and for planning.

It must be noted that, given Holland's objectives, his tactics are rather odd. The book is presented as an attack on Crosland's revisionism expressed in *The Future of Socialism*. But if the intention is to convert the revisionists the tone is far too hostile; it appears instead to be written for the left, who already believe in public ownership. It is thus unlikely to shift moderate opinion in the Labour Party while it could well be rejected as too generous to capitalism by the left.

Although there is considerable discussion of planning in *The Socialist Challenge*, the case for it is assumed rather than argued. Holland's main concern is with the changes that are needed to make it effective. His starting point is the assumption that government intervention is needed to achieve the macro-economic objectives of full employment, price stability, a satisfactory balance of payments and an adequate growth of real incomes. His central argument is that the post-war Keynesian approach to these problems is inadequate.

THE MESOECONOMY AND KEYNESIAN POLICIES

The failure of Keynesian policies is explained by the increasing dominance of the economy by large multi-national corporations. The size of these corporations allows them to avoid the pressures and constraints of market competition; their multi-national character allows them to avoid or frustrate the directives and policies of national governments. Holland calls this sector the 'mesoeconomy'. It stands between the micro-economy of classical economics and the macro-economy of Keynesian economics. The emergence of the mesoeconomy means that the Keynesian approach to the management of the economy, in which the government aims to control the economic aggregates – output, employment, inflation, etc – mainly by regulating total demand, while leaving the market to allocate resources at the micro-level, will no longer work. Holland claims that a new set of instruments is needed. They include direct government intervention in the mesoeconomy by acquiring a number of leading companies – perhaps twenty to twenty-five – within it.

He argues that the ideas of Keynesian economic management would be perfectly adequate if only the world still consisted of competitive firms which were tied to national markets and which had short investment horizons. He suggests that this world was already disappearing as Keynes wrote *The General Theory*, and that the rise of the mesoeconomy has destroyed it completely. Keynesian intervention has failed to achieve economic growth; it has failed to achieve price stability; it has failed to solve the balance of payments problem; it has failed to avoid stop-go; it has failed to achieve full employment.

Holland analyses the failure of Keynesian theory in terms of the objectives of economic policy. The traditional post-war approach to the objective of full employment has been to manage overall demand by varying government expenditure and personal taxation – including changes in direct taxes – by changing investment and employment incentives, and by changing the cost and availability of credit. There has also been direct regulation – for example, industrial development certificates. Holland argues that although changes in government expenditure and personal taxation may have the required effects on total demand, at least in the short run, they fail to generate the desired second-round effects on industrial investment. In other words, the government may be able to increase the level of consumers' expenditure by cutting taxes, but companies do not respond by increasing investment. The other measures, which are intended to act directly on investment, do not work either. There are two general reasons for this. Companies do not believe that the government will be able to sustain the level of demand; they fear that the government's inability to solve the balance-of-payments problem will lead inevitably to 'stop' after a brief period of 'go'. The other general reason is that the mesoeconomy is able to avoid the effects of investment policies. For example, if credit is tight in the UK, the multi-nationals can acquire credit from abroad. If the government tries to direct the location of investment through industrial development certificates, the multi-nationals can threaten to move production abroad. The failure to achieve adequate economic growth is similarly explained, with particular emphasis on the failure to achieve a high enough level of investment.

The failure to achieve full employment, the failure to achieve high growth and the failure to avoid stop-go depend in the end on the failure to solve the balance-of-payments problem. Holland's explanation for the persistence of the balance-of-payments problem is based principally on the question of 'transfer pricing'. A large multi-national company will usually be transferring goods and services from one national branch or subsidiary to another. The prices 'charged' by one branch to another will affect recorded profits and hence the company's tax liability. Given the freedom to do so, the multi-national company will set its transfer prices in such a way that its total tax bill is minimized. Holland argues that since the UK has been a relatively highly taxed country, transfer pricing has put a permanent strain on our balance of payments.

The problem of transfer pricing is well recognized by the Inland Revenue, and energetic steps are taken to minimize abuses, although they are admittedly not completely successful. Also, the UK has since become something of a company tax haven. Further, it is extremely important to distinguish between the movements of funds across the national exchanges, which may cause a problem, and book-keeping entries in company accounts which do not. Movements of funds by multi-nationals can

127

cause short-run balance-of-payments problems, but that has nothing to do with transfer pricing as such.

The final area of policy failure blamed on the mesoeconomy is the control of inflation. Holland argues that the lack of competitive pressure gives the mesoeconomy freedom of price-setting. It uses this power to achieve a high rate of inflation. Furthermore, it is extremely difficult for the government to check this process, since transfer pricing conceals the firm's true cost structure.

Thus the mesoeconomy frustrates policies for growth and full employment because it fails to invest at home; it frustrates policies to improve the balance of payments by its transfer pricing and overseas investment, and it frustrates attempts to control inflation because it can exercise monopoly power. Holland argues that active intervention in the mesoeconomy would restore successful policymaking to the government. By a combination of direct ownership and the use of planning agreements, it would ensure adequate investment; it would provide sufficient direct knowledge of cost structures to expose bogus transfer pricing, and it would restore competitive pricing in domestic markets.

Holland's account of the failure of Keynesian economics is familiar; his explanation is new, though reminiscent of the pre-war concern with monopoly. An alternative explanation, given in Chapter 2, is that the government's ability to control either the level of employment or the rate of growth is limited, and that inflation and balance-of-payments problems have been caused by its attempts to operate the economy at too high a pressure of demand. Holland's explanation, if it is correct, is far more optimistic since it implies that the performance of the economy can be improved by fairly minor institutional changes. There must, however, be grave doubts about his analysis, since it is based on a long list of things the multi-nationals could do rather than on a list of things they are likely to want to do or have been doing. Further, it does not satisfactorily explain why the UK's economic performance is relatively so poor, since multi-nationals operate in all non-communist economies.

The main charge against the mesoeconomy is that it does not invest enough, and lack of investment, according to Holland, has been the main cause of our problems: '. . . the basis of the crisis lies in the underlying failure of our leading firms to invest on a sufficient scale in this country to generate income and demand from which they too can benefit through high and sustained sales.'[6] Thus if the investment were carried out, the required demand for additional output would, apparently, be generated. Under the present system of demand management, it is not possible to achieve higher investment, but a combination of planning agreements and vigorous investment policies in the state-owned part of dynamic industries would cause a general increase in investment. With these instruments, the government will be able to plan effectively.

Put more simply, it can plan for the medium to long term and avoid the main waves of the stop-go cycle. This should make it possible for a low-growth economy such as Britain's to achieve a higher growth path, and make sure that a higher proportion of the entirely new plant forthcoming from higher growth is located in problem regions and areas.[7]

That is very like the kind of 'virtuous circle' assumption used in connection with the NEDC and National Plan experiments, with the important difference that the government will generate the investment by its activities in the mesoeconomy. The National Plan failed, he argued, because 'It was a plan for the transformation of the economy through mobilizing private enterprise in the public interest.'[8]

Holland's analysis leads him to the conclusion that a major expansion of the public sector through the National Enterprise Board, and control over the private sector by the use of planning agreements, are necessary conditions for a 'successful planning strategy'. It is not clear what the strategy consists of, apart from a general need to in-

129

crease investment. There is no discussion of how investment plans are to be coordinated, except to the extent that the planning agreements will involve an exchange of information with the government. But those, presumably, are details to be worked out with experience.

FROM THEORY TO POLICY

Full proposals for the National Enterprise Board were set out in an Opposition Green Paper, published in 1972.[9] Holland was a member of the study group that produced it, and the proposals and arguments closely followed those in his book. The Green Paper stated: 'We now propose that the next Labour Government urgently sets up a large and powerful National Enterprise Board to introduce public ownership into the strongholds of private industry.' The role of the Board in economic planning was stressed. For effective planning, it was necessary to spread the Board's holdings throughout industry.

> Firms in any given sector are strongly influenced by the investment planning, plant building, and pricing policies of their most feared competitor (not necessarily the largest firm in the sector). Fear of losing their share of the market can be a more effective stimulus than the wise words of government.

The Board would make planning effective because its role in 'the new commanding heights of the modern capitalist economy' would allow the government's intentions to be carried out directly. In addition, there would be a 'pull' effect on private companies, who would either be competing with NEB controlled companies, or selling their goods to them. 'In this way, the previous gap between the economic plans of the government and the actual policies pursued in the private sector, would be more effectively bridged than in the 1965 National Plan.'

The next stage in the development of policy was *Labour's Programme 1973*, prepared for the 1973 Party

Conference. It included a section on economic planning, which was based on the NEC document on the National Enterprise Board. It started: 'A massive shift is needed in the social and regional distribution of growth. And this can only be achieved by a conscious effort to *plan* the economy.' The key to their planning effort was the domination of the economy by a few leading firms. 'We will harness directly the energies of these giants – leaving the numerous smaller firms to our more general planning policies.' They stated two points of principle; first, that their intervention would concern strategy, not tactics; second, 'that we will not attempt to meet precisely a set of over-detailed economic targets or expect to bring about a miraculous spurt in economic growth'. As can be seen, it was necessary to distinguish the present exercise from the National Plan.

The basis of planning was to rest on three major pillars, each of which was essential to its success. The first was new public enterprise and, especially, the creation of a state holding company 'to establish a major public stake in manufacturing industry'. The second was the planning agreements system, 'a completely new system, which will place all our dealing with the major companies onto a systematic and coherent basis.' The third was a new Industry Act, 'to provide the next Labour Government with all the industrial powers it will need to meet its economic objectives.'

The discussion of the new public enterprise was provided in a revealing section on the public sector. The introduction to the section said:

There are many strands of socialist analysis and belief which throughout the history of our movement have made the theme of the public ownership of our national industrial resources central to the achievement of a socialist society. At a time when the advance of technology has raised the stakes, and when the economic power which ownership carried with it has become more concentrated in fewer hands, they have never been more relevant.

131

The document then went on to discuss the purposes of public ownership. The first was the need to transfer economic power 'from a small elite to the mass of the people', in order to achieve equality. As far as the second major purpose was concerned,

> The experience of the last ten years has shown very clearly that economic planning in the national interest has been continuously frustrated by the inability to exercise effective control over those vital economic processes which determine our national well-being. In particular, the level of investment in industry has shown itself to be highly resistant to incentives, exhortations and the limited measures of control over private industry which are at the disposal of Governments.

It went on:

> It is now plainly evident that private and public interests do not by any means always coincide, and that only direct control, through ownership, of a substantial and vital sector of the growth industries, mainly in manufacturing, which hold the key to investment performance, will allow a Labour Government of the future to achieve its essential planning objectives in the national interest. An expanded public sector is a key instrument of the planning process.

This seems to be a striking victory, both for the analysis of *The Socialist Challenge* and even for pre-war socialist thought. The main difference is that whereas before the war it was argued that market capitalism could not achieve full employment, now it is argued that it could not achieve rapid economic growth.

The planning agreements system was expected to cover the largest one hundred or so manufacturing firms together with all public enterprises. The objectives included: the exchange of information; the use of information so acquired to determine the national planning objectives; the agreement by firms to help the government meet certain objectives; the provision of a basis for channelling selective government assistance to those firms 'which agree to help us meet the nation's planning objectives'. The Industry Act was to provide the power needed for the new system of planning. It would allow the next Labour Government to act 'swiftly and *selectively*, directly at the level of the firm'.

The subsequent manifestoes, prepared for the two elections of 1974, kept to the general policies proposed in *Labour's Programme 1973*. The manifesto for October 1974, *Britain will Win with Labour*, said that the Industry Act would provide for a system of planning agreements with key companies to ensure that the plans of those companies 'are in harmony with national needs and objectives'. The National Enterprise Board would be set up 'to extend public ownership into profitable manufacturing industry by acquisitions, partly or wholly, of individual firms; to stimulate investment; to create employment in areas of high unemployment; to encourage industrial democracy; to promote industrial efficiency.'

The Socialist Challenge had thus become the basis of a radical programme which once again put public ownership and planning at the centre of the party's programme. It involved a new theory – the power of the multinationals – and a new system of planning, direct public ownership of profitable industry plus planning agreements with key companies. It also involved methods whereby the Labour Party's commitment to industrial democracy could be made effective. It remains to be seen what success it will have in practice, if, indeed, it is put into action.

In the course of translating the proposals into specific policies, there has been an important shift in emphasis. The emphasis now is not so much on commanding the vigour of the mesoeconomy as on breathing life into moribund industry. A key idea is the attempt to reverse 'the de-industrialisation of society', the decline in the manufacturing sector of the economy. It was first emphasized by Tony Benn, who, in an article in *Trade and Industry* on 4 April 1974, talked of the fall in employment in manufacturing industry and saw it leading to a 'continuing shutdown of British industry, low wages, rising unemployment and the emigration of our skilled workers', together with balance-of-payments problems and social decay. The theme was continued in a White Paper on *The Regeneration of British Industry*,[10] published in August 1974.

It matters vitally to all of us that British industry should be strong and successful. We need both efficient publicly-owned industries, and a vigorous, alert, responsible and profitable private sector, working together with the Government in a framework which brings together the interests of all concerned.

It commented that investment per worker was less than half that in France, Japan and the United States, and that while domestic investment stagnated, direct investment overseas by British firms in the previous ten years had more than trebled.

The White Paper described the system of planning agreements and the proposed role of the National Enterprise Board.

The Government propose to create a new instrument to secure where necessary large-scale sustained investment to offset the effects of the short-term pull of market forces. These new powers of initiative are better exercised through a new agency than dealt with directly by the Government, and for this purpose it is proposed to set up a National Enterprise Board (NEB).

It set out its responsibilities and said: 'Its main strength in manufacturing will come through the extension of public ownership into profitable manufacturing industry by acquisitions of individual firms.' The necessary powers for the establishment of the NEB and the introduction of planning agreements were duly incorporated in the Industry Act 1975.

The Act fell some way short of the National Executive Committee's original proposals, as they complained somewhat bitterly in *Labour and Industry: the Next Steps*, presented to the Annual Conference of 1975. They criticized the Act's proposals that planning agreements were to be voluntary, that capital grants were not to be channelled through them, and that they would not be tied up explicitly with price controls. They complained further that there were no powers for the compulsory purchase of companies, except in the case of foreign takeover, and that the funds provided for the NEB were inadequate.

The National Executive Committee made a renewed call for a national plan. They admitted past failures but claimed to have learnt much from them:

> Our proposed new plan would rely not on out-of-date information, or on exhortation at national and industrial level – but on face-to-face contact with big companies, backed by new industrial powers, new public enterprise, and the involvement of trade unionists. There would, moreover, be nothing rigid about the new Plan: it would respond swiftly to the continuing flow of information – and especially information gleaned from Planning Agreements and from the regions.

They called for a specialized planning unit within the government machine, which would be staffed not only by career civil servants, who in many cases 'will lack any real commitment to making the Plan a success', but by specialists 'able to negotiate as *equals* with their counterparts in industry'.

But government policy shifted, if anything even further from the National Executive Committee's proposals. Tony Benn, who had become a bogeyman, was replaced as Secretary of State for Industry by Eric Varley. The move was seen as a sop to industry and, possibly, to the international financial community. Both planning agreements and the positive role of the NEB were played down and emphasis was shifted to Industrial Strategy.

A paper setting out the government's views, 'An

Approach to Industrial Strategy', was presented to the NEDC on 5 November 1975 and published in *Trade and Industry* on 7 November 1975. The analysis it contained 'does not itself constitute a strategy; it provides a flexible framework within which strategic decisions can be made'. The paper argued that instruments such as planning agreements and the NEB could only be useful if there was a 'soundly based strategy for manufacturing industry'. The paper set out the government's approach to the development of such a strategy.

The paper listed twelve factors which might explain the poor performance of manufacturing industry. They included: low and inefficient investment, inadequate development of manpower policy, sharp and frequent changes in government policy, excessive public expenditure, interference with nationalized industries, declining industrial profitability, imperfections in the capital markets mainly at the medium- and longer-term ends, a capital market which does not give priority to the needs of industry.

The elements of an Industrial Strategy would include: better coordination of industrial policies, more effective use of industrial policy instruments ('Both planning agreements and the NEB will be important here'); sufficient profits and adequate finance for investment, better manpower policy; improved planning based on tripartite discussion and on greater disclosure of information at company level, 'particularly, but not exclusively, in planning agreements'.

The paper considered the possibility of a new national plan:

One response to the problem might be for the Government to set in hand a new National Plan. The likelihood is that any plan which erected a single complete and mutually consistent set of industrial forecasts and targets would rapidly be falsified by events and have to be discarded. This would once again discredit the process of industrial planning in this country as did previous attempts which failed largely because they were based on unsustainable economic assumptions, and paid too little attention to the constraints affecting individual industries and companies.

This time a more flexible approach was to be adopted. The likely prospects of the most important sectors of industry over the next five years would be considered, and their role in meeting overall economic objectives would be indicated. The paper set out the procedure which would normally move through three stages each year. The first stage would be the presentation of the government's medium-term projections, a paper identifying those industries where action might be needed, and detailed analysis of industries, drawing attention to strong and weak points. The second stage would be discussion of the detailed figures by the EDCs. In the third stage (at about the turn of the year), a report based on the EDC discussions would be submitted to NEDC.

This report would then form the basis for an important discussion by the council on industrial policy in general, and in particular on areas highlighted for action and improvement, at a time of the year suitable for influencing the Government's thinking on macro-economic policy.

The implied promise is that the report would be taken into account in the preparation of the Budget.

The first stage of the Industrial Strategy was completed by August 1976, when the report of the Industrial Strategy Staff Group was presented to NEDC. The report was based on the work of nearly forty working parties. The government welcomed the report: 'The first stage of the work has in fact been far more successful than might have been expected. It certainly justifies us in going on to a second.' In a paper to NEDC, the Chancellor of the Exchequer and the Secretary of State for Industry said: 'More generally, the Government are committed to promoting a profitable and vigorous private sector aspect of our mixed economy, and to giving greater priority to industry over consumption or even our social objectives.'

The subsequent history of the Industrial Strategy has not been so encouraging. At the NEDC meeting of 4 August 1976, the council was offered two alternative growth 'scenarios' to 1979. One was based on 'Past Trends', ie the kind of growth actually achieved in the past; the other was based on 'Improved Industrial Performance'. On the basis of past trends, the growth of total output was projected to grow by 3.3 per cent a year between 1975 and 1979. (This was itself considerably over-optimistic.) On the basis of 'Improved Industrial Performance', total output was projected to grow by 4.6 per cent a year over the same period. Exports, in the first case, would grow at 9.6 per cent a year; in the second case, they would grow at 12 per cent a year. The council unanimously accepted the 'Improved Industrial Performance' case as the basis for its future work. It had apparently learnt nothing at all from history.

THE POLITICS OF THE INDUSTRIAL STRATEGY

The Labour Party would like to offer planning as its particular approach to economic policy, but it has twice abandoned it: the first time while nobody noticed; the second time amidst the glare of publicity. It is naturally cautious about a third attempt. The Industrial Strategy is carefully distinguished from the National Plan: the approach is company by company rather than industry by industry or in terms of grandiose national targets. In principle it should be a flexible system, allowing for rapid response to changing world markets.

So far the Industrial Strategy has been a slogan rather than a set of practical measures. Its advantage in being so vague is its appeal to a wide range of Labour supporters. It has lost all the teeth with which the left wanted to arm it, yet it is still recognizably descended from Stuart Holland's theories. There is nothing in it to frighten away moderate supporters of the Labour Party, yet after three years of Labour Government no planning agreement has been signed, and the National Enterprise Board is identified with rescue operations, such as that of British Leyland, rather than with thrusting profitable enterprise. Why has the performance lagged so far behind the promises, modest as they were? Part of the explanation lies in current economic conditions. The problems of inflation, in particular, have absorbed the government's energies. Success in controlling inflation was seen as the first political need, and the government has been prepared to accept a very high cost in terms of unemployment in the attempt to achieve it. Promises of a more prosperous future might have been regarded as diversionary tactics designed to distract attention from current problems. Further, the extreme difficulty of knowing how rapidly Britain could return to a more normal growth of output combined with uncertainties about international trade produces severe practical problems in drawing up any planning agreement. Finally, there has been a period of severe cuts in public expenditure together with stringent control of the money supply, which limits the scope both for industrial aid and for acquiring companies.

The reluctance to use the Industrial Strategy strenuously must also be due to fears about political feasibility. As a vague proposal it has a challenging but inoffensive ring; as a set of policy measures it could be strongly opposed. The Conservatives opposed the Industry Act vigorously, particularly over the measures which proposed government intervention and wider dissemination of company information. In a precarious international financial situation it was probably feared that the much publicized threat of bare-faced socialism linked with the Act and with the politics of Benn was too much of a danger to sterling, quite apart from what it might have done to British industry.

Even when the fears of a sterling crisis have passed, the government knows that the public is in general opposed to further nationalization and it is unclear that it would recognize the Act's proposals as a new and improved variety. One suspects that the value of the Industrial

Strategy is its very vagueness: people feel that the decline in British industry must be bad; a policy to reverse it must be desirable. The quest for industries with high growth potential seems pragmatic and refreshingly non-doctrinaire. The combination of company planning and improved industrial relations seems highly attractive. The general feeling of goodwill could be rapidly dissipated in the face of serious policy proposals.

Chapter 8: The Future of Planning

This account of planning has covered a period of nearly sixty years from the Labour Party's manifesto of 1918 to the Industrial Strategy of 1976. In terms of ideas the story ends remarkably close to where it started, though there have been quite large diversions on the way.

The Labour Party began by asserting that market capitalism was immoral. It subsequently argued that market capitalism was inefficient, particularly in ensuring enough jobs for the workers. This was believed to be due partly to the widespread existence of monopolies, to which the solution was public ownership and planning. It is now argued that market capitalism is inefficient mainly in ensuring rapid economic growth but also in providing enough employment. This is said by the left to be due to the large multi-national companies which are free from the constraints of competition. The solution is public ownership and planning.

The Conservatives have not consistently supported or opposed planning. They supported one version of it before the war and supported another version of it in the early 1960s. At other periods they opposed planning strongly. They have not, on the other hand, been great advocates of market forces. The Tory tradition, personified by such men as Macmillan, has been extremely sceptical about them. When they have advocated planning, it has been within a framework of private capitalism, but they have not been dogmatic opponents of all nationalization.

In the 1950s there was a period in which both parties generally agreed that government intervention could be limited to the management of demand by manipulation of fiscal and monetary policy. The rest could be left to the market. At the end of the 1950s it was felt that such policies had not successfully stabilized output and were preventing growth. Hence the call for a new approach to demand management and the introduction of a new style of planning. That experiment failed and was followed by a period of yet more restrictive demand management. A promise by the Conservative Government of 1970 to reduce the scope of government intervention was soon broken. Fiscal and monetary policies were used strenuously in an attempt to expand demand while incomes policies were used in an attempt – which proved vain – to control inflation. The most recent development sees the return of a modified form of planning. Its positive side is the capturing 'in the public interest' of the dynamism of some of the most profitable firms in manufacturing industry. Under 'planning agreements', their strategy will be directed to raising the rate of economic growth and reducing regional disparities. Its other aspect is the attempt to stem or reverse what Tony Benn has called 'the devastating trend to contraction in British industry,' – or 'de-industrialization'.

At the same time, there is again a disillusion with conventional methods of demand management. In some ways this is more severe than in the late 1950s. At least then it was generally agreed that the government could control output, even if when it did so its timing was wrong and it paid too much attention to the balance of payments; but current attitudes are much more sceptical. It is no longer believed that we can 'spend our way out of a depression'.

The reaction of the left to this disillusion has been to call for more intervention. In particular, our difficulties have been blamed on our vulnerability to foreign competition. Import controls have been proposed as a solution to the problem. A further argument (not confined to the left) has been that the low level of investment has been caused by a failure of the financial institutions to direct funds towards manufacturing investment. The proposed solutions have varied from nationalization of the banks to the creation of new institutions (such as Finance for Industry) which are intended to remedy alleged defects in the present financial system. Against this, the liberal reaction (confusingly described as extreme right) has been to call for greater reliance on market forces, not only in decisions about production and consumption but also in the management of demand. The extreme case states that the government ought not to attempt to control the level of output in the economy at all.

It is argued as follows: there is no reason to believe that the government is better at forecasting the future than anyone else. For example, businessmen will be able to foresee a world depression as well as the government and they will know how it will affect their activity. If output and employment are to be maintained, they will need to switch their output from foreign to domestic markets. If they do not do this and instead allow output and employment to fall, this is their rational choice and reflects the costs of adjusting from one market to another. If the government intervenes, for example by cutting taxes to increase consumers' expenditure or by increasing public expenditure, it merely distorts the economy and makes it less able to deal with the next recovery of world trade.

This extreme case, associated with the idea of 'rational expectations', would leave the government with a minimal role in the management of the economy and would require it only to maintain prudent control over the money supply (preferably according to pre-determined rules).

Between the extremes of interventionism and liberalism, the short-run management of the economy has moved away from reliance on changes in fiscal policy to maintain the level of demand and employment towards a broader framework of financial and monetary guidelines; but the belief remains that intervention should be used to reverse de-industrialization and increase the rate of economic growth.

What will be the future of planning? One can answer fairly confidently that it will be much the same as its past. Planning will occasionally swing into favour, not because of any virtues it has or is believed to have but because it can be presented as better than whatever the current experiment in demand management is. It is now more likely to be introduced by the left than by the right because the Labour Party has an ideological tendency to believe in public ownership and a tactical desire to propose a distinct approach to economic policy.

One can also predict fairly confidently that experiments in planning will be muddled failures. The reason is that economic planning in Britain ignores the role of market forces both in its diagnosis of the problem and in its proposed solutions. At least this is consistent, but it is consistently wrong. The government could make planning effective if it were prepared to introduce adequate direct controls, but this too is contrary to the British tradition. The government has to rely heavily on such methods as indicative planning and moral exhortation, neither of which is effective when major changes in structure are required.

The dilemma is well illustrated by the concern with de-industrialization and slow economic growth. Why should de-industrialization be a cause for concern? Tony Benn has written: 'It is no exaggeration to say that Britain's whole future depends upon major investment in the expansion and re-equipment of our manufacturing plants aimed at restoring British industry to a competitive position in world and home markets.'[1] Such an investment programme would involve doubling the annual rate of investment in manufacturing, much more rapid growth of output than in the past, intense planning and adequate funds. 'The human task of organizing such a recovery programme would impose a very heavy strain on all those concerned. While the investment cost would be large, it is one which as a nation we have to afford.'

Why should this heavy burden be imposed on us? It seems to be taken as axiomatic that de-industrialization is a bad thing. Market forces are causing a steady decline in industrial employment. The evidence suggests that it is increasingly difficult for manufacturing industry to find profitable markets either at home or abroad. This has happened in spite of generous subsidies and tax concessions. Why should one try to maintain, or even expand, manufacturing industry under these circumstances? It has been suggested that one reason for the decline has been that the pressure of demand for labour in the public sector has pushed up real wages everywhere and made it unprofitable for manufacturing industry to maintain its level of employment. But that is only a mistake if we have over-expanded the public sector to the point where the additional benefit from public sector employment is lower than the additional benefit from manufacturing sector employment. Unless that has happened it would be quite wrong to cut public sector employment just in order to expand the manufacturing sector.

Is it believed that the social returns from manufacturing are greater than the private returns? This is an accepted ground for intervention, but one rarely hears the case argued in these terms. There is certainly recognition of the social costs of closing down a firm or an industry; but that should determine the speed and the method of closure, it is not an argument for expanding industry. The best argument for attempting to expand industrialization in opposition to market signals is the 'infant industry argument' which claims that new industries should be allowed to develop behind a barrier of protection; but that can hardly be a case for the general expansion of industry.

In practice, the call for the regeneration of industry is axiomatic rather than reasoned. It appears to be based on a conviction that 'true wealth' must reside in manufacturing industry. At its worst it is combined with the view that the structure of output must never change. (It is ironic that Lewis, in his *Principles of Economic Planning*, assumed that the main function of planning was to accelerate structural change.) There is nothing either in economic theory or in economic history which suggests that prosperity need be based on manufacturing industry. It is not suggested that we should run down our manufacturing industries, but many of our special skills lie in the service sector, where there can be and have been considerable opportunities for increases in productivity. The truth is that no one can sit in an office in Whitehall and decide how large our manufacturing sector ought to be. If market forces are currently suggesting a decline that should be regarded as a valuable guide to what should be happening, even if it is important to reduce the hardship arising from such changes. An equally important objective is to ensure that we have as much market information as possible so that there should always be a preference for the provision of goods and services through the market rather than through public administration.

An associated view, which again relies on axiom rather than reason, is that Britain needs more engineers. It is frequently combined with the argument that it is wrong that engineers should be paid less than (say) accountants or salesmen. The solution usually proposed is to expand yet again university engineering places. (Since students, whose career depends on it, are possibly more clearsighted than administrators, the places are usually unfilled.) Any faith in markets would suggest that society places smaller value on engineers than on accountants, and that if anything there is an excess supply of the former. That may be distressing but the case for ignoring such market information has to be argued, not just taken for granted.

The important point is that if the government wishes to oppose these market signals, it will, in the case of deindustrialization, have to use massive powers of direction or incentive to reverse them. There is no question of using the former and it is unlikely to provide enough funds for the latter. In their place we have NEDC acclaiming projections which bear no resemblance to anything we have achieved in the past.

As a further example of the muddled approach to planning we can consider the question of investment. It plays an important role in the Industrial Strategy both as a means of ending the contraction of industry and as a means of increasing the growth rate. It will be recalled that the low level of investment is a major feature of Holland's argument in *The Socialist Challenge*. Again the market signal is that investment is unprofitable. Why should the signal be ignored? We have seen that throughout the history of economic planning, investment has most frequently been a candidate for intervention. First because it was believed there was too much; now because

it is believed there is too little. The case for more investment seems to be so generally accepted that it may seem
that all the arguments point unequivocally in that direction. It is therefore worth examining them carefully.

There may be a general argument in favour of encouraging investment and growth if the general weight of
policy (towards, for example, taxation and social security)
is unintentionally against it. This argument is accepted
for example by Paish, who is no intervener.[2] It would
provide grounds for subsidizing investment through taxation or by some other means. However there is a general
feeling (shared, it will be recalled, by Keynes) that investment cannot be left to the market. There is a profound
distrust of the workings of capital markets, which has two
elements. The first is that it is believed to be inefficient
even for those in whose interests it is supposed to operate;
the second is that it serves the interests of the wrong
people. The first element is particularly associated with a
dislike of the Stock Exchange.

The market for shares, it is generally agreed, has most
of the properties one would associate with a perfect market. It is mainly a secondary market, that is it is concerned
with the exchange of existing shares rather than the issue
of new shares. But the resulting level of share prices provides a guide to the required private return on capital investment. The required return will vary with the fluctuations in share prices. High share prices will encourage
investment, low share prices will discourage it. This behaviour is regarded as irrational. For example, Holland
talks of 'the irrationality of a stock market which failed
to invest in manufacturing industry and killed off profits,
plus inefficient management continuing to claim up to the
moment of bankruptcy that public enterprise will ruin the
country.'[3]

Management may be inefficient (though it is not clear
where public enterprise will get more efficient managers
from) but there is so much confusion about the role of
the stock market that it is hard to know where to begin.
It was industry which failed to invest in industry. It could
always have raised funds on the stock market (at a price)

if it wanted to, but it chose not to do so. It chose not to do so because it feared that there were no prospects of earning adequate profits. (The stock market cannot possibly 'kill off profits', although governments can help to do so.)

As far as the interests of holders of capital are concerned, the evidence supports the view that financial markets operate efficiently in their interests. That is not to deny that mistakes are made. In a world of uncertainty that is inevitable, and there is no reason to believe that the government will make fewer mistakes.

The belief that the government should intervene to increase the rate of investment, in spite of market signals, must be based either on some view of a discrepancy between social returns and private returns, or on a political judgement that even if the market correctly records people's preferences, those preferences should be ignored. Again, one rarely hears the argument discussed in these terms. We have already suggested that the tax system may have discouraged saving and investment; but it would seem easier to change the tax system. One version of the case for over-riding the capital market's preferences is that the market is unrepresentative, since only capitalists of one type or another are represented there. Against this it could be argued that the relevant part of the community is that part which actually does the saving. Further, the 'non-representativeness' argument should lead if anything to less investment not more, since those who do not save are prepared to pay very high rates of interest indeed (usually through hire purchase) in order to borrow. Their behaviour suggests that more resources should be allocated towards consumption rather than towards investment.

In practice, no such arguments are considered. High investment is a Good Thing and must be encouraged. But as with de-industrialization, the government does not arm itself with the weapons to oppose market forces on such a large scale. As Roger Opie said of the National Plan, '. . . there was no question of e.g. cheap finance for investment necessary for the Plan . . . or the denial of finance to certain industries or firms in order to concentrate resources in the "worthy" industries or firms.'[4]

In Britain it is usually safe to assume that tomorrow will be much like today. There is no reason to believe that we shall escape from the present compromise. We shall not move far either towards intervention or the market. Extreme interventionism in the form of wholehearted socialist or capitalist planning would contradict our historical traditions. When a speaker at a Conservative Party conference is able to end his speech with thunderous applause by referring to the Red Flag as the flag of 'an alien creed' he is not just appealing to the ill-informed prejudices of his audience; he is referring to the historical truth that Britain has avoided extremes both of left and right. This has resulted largely from the conditions under which first commerce and then industrialization were grafted onto England's developing class system.[5] (The extreme left would argue that capitalist planning is ruled out because of the capitalists' fear that an effective planning system might fall into the hands of the workers.)

It can, however, be argued that there will be a steady drift away from the market. This will happen because the call from the left, who are the main supporters of planning, is not resisted by the centre. An important, and possibly dominant group of the centre combines the Tory traditions of benevolent leadership with the Fabian tradition of meritocratic paternalism. (The word 'Fabian' is used to cover a wider range of people, and a narrower range of ideas, than would normally be associated with membership of the Fabian Society.) These two groups have dominated politics and, more importantly, the Civil Service since before the war.

This is not a conspiracy theory. What one might call the 'caring middle classes' are a major source of decency and humanity. But the result has been an excessive fear of market forces and a reluctance to use them to solve economic problems. They are encouraged in this by both businessmen and trade unions who have no particular desire to encourage market competition.

One cynical explanation for this mistrust of markets would be that greater reliance on the market would reduce the role of both politicians and civil servants. But one must recognize that it is altruism, mistaken though it may be, which leads to intervention. Important elements include a determination to avoid the miseries of the 1930s, a desire to protect the weak, and an idea that there is a long list of difficulties about the workings of the market system, as indeed there is, but the central question is not the length of the list but its importance.

If a sharp move either towards intervention or towards the market is unlikely, there is now an alternative means of trying to resolve our economic difficulties. There is a move towards tripartite discussions (between government, unions and employers) in which it is hoped to get agreement on policies, for example, to control inflation and reduce unemployment. The discussion may simply be between government and unions. It is described as 'corporatism', a name which has had far more sinister association in pre-war Germany and Italy, but which has also been applied to the system (true of pre-war Britain) in which the organization of planning is left in the hands of industrial monopolies and cartels. It is, as F. A. Hayek has said, 'a state of affairs which can satisfy neither planners nor liberals . . . This is the inevitable first result of a situation in which the people are united in their hostility to competition but agree on little else.'[6]

Alarm calls have, rightly, been sounded about the approach of the Corporate State. It threatens to avoid the democratic controls both of the market and of parliament. It is likely to fail as a method of solving our economic problems since too little is known about the economy for there to be workable bargains in terms of promises by the government of output and promises by the unions for wage restraint. The chances are that whatever is agreed upon will not be feasible, and one side or another will withdraw having seen the promises broken. It would be better still if the experiment were not attempted: one can have no faith in a process of bargaining which so ill-represents the interests of most citizens.

FROM CONVENTIONAL PLANNING TO STRATEGIC
PLANNING

Is there any escape from the drift to planning? Even if
people could not agree that it is undesirable, they might
at least be persuaded that it is impractical. It is worth
quoting again the cautionary note in the Labour Government's Long-term Programme of 1948:

> Economic planning in the United Kingdom is based
> upon three fundamental facts: the economic fact that
> the United Kingdom economy must be heavily depen-
> dent upon international trade; the political fact that it
> is, and intends to remain, a democratic nation, with a
> high degree of individual liberty; and the administrative
> fact that no economic planning body can be aware (or
> indeed ever could be aware) of more than the very
> general trends of future economic developments.

Have any of these facts changed? Britain is more dependent than ever on international trade; it retains, one
hopes, its commitment to democracy and individual
liberty, and recent experiences have shown how little ability we have to foresee economic developments. The difficulties of planning have increased, and make the need for
a flexible response to changing conditions more important than ever.

Further, one must recognize the shifts of power required to make planning effective. Medium- and long-
term plans, as usually conceived, subordinate the present
to the future. Such plans impose completely new types
of limit on politicians and officials. Would they really be
prepared to sacrifice their current taste for short-term
measures, particularly where economic policy is concerned, to longer-term objectives? This is not to deny
that parliament can and does take decisions with vital
long-term implications, but the nature of decision-taking
and of the political debate emphasizes the immediate at
the expense of the long-term. Experience also suggests

that the unions would be reluctant to sacrifice their short-term bargaining power in return for planning.

All these difficulties provide further explanations of why attempts at planning, even if they were desirable, are likely to fail. One can argue that the present system concentrates far too much on tactics and not enough on strategy. Indeed, it is this emphasis on tactics which has made it so difficult for governments to recognize the constraints within which they operate, and sends them off from time to time in pursuit of a plan which they hope will solve everything.

C. E. Lindblom offers a possible solution in his paper, 'The Sociology of Planning: Thought and Social Interaction'.[7] He distinguishes between the 'intellectually guided society' and the 'preference guided society'. In the former, it is believed that the application of reason can determine how society should be organized. In the latter, decision-taking is decentralized and institutions are formed by social interaction, not by reason. The intellectually guided society is most akin to an ideal type of totalitarian society; the preference guided society is most akin to an ideal type of liberal democracy. 'Politics abounds in the preference ordered society.' The market is its characteristic institution. The preference guided society relies on interaction to produce solutions to its problems, not because they will be perfect but because they will often be superior to those attempted by the intellect.

Lindblom is saying something rather different from extreme liberals such as Milton Friedman. He defends interaction and markets less for their political value than for their ability to solve problems. 'Personal liberty is valued, not simply for its own sake or on humanitarian grounds, but for its function in stretching society's meagre resources of intellect in solving its basic problems.' Lindblom points out that the style of economic planning (which he labels 'conventional planning') adopted in liberal democracies is based on a set of ideas close to those of the intellectually guided society. It is an alien intrusion into liberal democratic society. He proposes instead the idea of 'strategic planning' which is cautious in selecting its tasks and makes much use of interaction: 'A conventional planner would be willing directly to tackle the task of resource allocation for an entire economy; a strategic planner would not.'[8]

Strategic planning resembles the style of planning undertaken by companies in competitive markets. They recognize that their control over the environment is limited, and develop a system for responding to market forces. They are negotiating with the environment rather than seeking to control it. The tasks of a strategic planner would include improving the efficiency of markets and encouraging their establishment where they currently do not exist. It would also include devising methods for the cheap distribution of information. In part, the planning experiments of the 1960s were exercises in strategic planning inasmuch as they sought to encourage industries to exchange information about their plans; but they were made to fit into a rigid framework of conventional planning which collapsed completely and had to be discarded when it encountered short-term problems.

Strategic planning presents its most important challenge to the Labour Party. The Labour Party has sought to further its worthy humanitarian ideals by central direction of the economy. The intentions have been excellent, but good intentions are not enough. Its attitude to economic policy has been guided by advisers whose arrogant elitism should never have been tolerated in any party which claimed to give power to the people. These policies have failed, and the reaction has been either to select scapegoats – monopolies, multi-national corporations, bankers at home and abroad – or to attempt to devise further instruments to control and regulate the economy. Its task should be to consider how its objectives could be met within a system which emphasizes the recognition of and response to individual demands rather than the efficient administration of centrally determined plans. An important part of this task is to consider how society can use markets while preserving the admirable human instinct for cooperation rather than conflict.

The impression that remains is that in the history of attitudes to planning, the political solutions have achieved the current compromise not because the case for the market has been defeated but because (with honourable exceptions) it has rarely been put.

Notes

1. INTRODUCTION

1. J. Leruez, *Economic Planning and Politics in Britain*; tr. M. Harrison (Martin Robertson, 1975), p. 1.
2. E. A. G. Robinson, *Economic Planning in the United Kingdom* (Cambridge University Press, 1967), p. 3.
3. R. Bailey, *Managing the British Economy* (Hutchinson, 1968), p. 9.
4. L. Robbins, *Planning and International Order* (Macmillan, 1937), p. 3.
5. J. K. Galbraith, *The New Industrial State* (Hamish Hamilton, 1967), p. 22.
6. J. Mitchell, *Groundwork to Economic Planning* (Secker & Warburg, 1966), p. 28.
7. S. Brittan, *Is There an Economic Consensus?* (Macmillan, 1973).
8. R. H. S. Crossman, 'Towards a Philosophy of Socialism', in *New Fabian Essays*; ed. R. H. S. Crossman (Turnstile Press, 1952).
9. W. L. S. Churchill, *Parliamentary Government and the Economic Problem* (Oxford University Press, 1930).

2. THE BACKGROUND TO THE DEBATE

1. S. Brittan, *Capitalism and the Permissive Society* (Macmillan, 1973), p. 87.
2. See, for example, F. A. Hayek, *The Road to Serfdom* (Routledge & Kegan Paul, 1944); and M. Friedman, *Capitalism and Freedom* (University of Chicago Press, 1962).
3. D. E. Moggridge, *Keynes* (Fontana, 1976).
4. J. M. Keynes, 'The End of Laissez-Faire', in *Essays in Persuasion* (Macmillan, 1931), p. 316.
5. *Ibid*, p. 316.

6. *Ibid*, p. 318.
7. J. M. Keynes, *The General Theory of Unemployment, Interest and Money* (Macmillan, 1936), p. 375.
8. *Ibid*, p. 378.
9. *Idem*.
10. *Ibid*, p. 380.
11. *Employment Policy* (Cmnd 6527, May 1944).
12. M. Friedman, *Capitalism and Freedom, op. cit.*' p. 9.
13. 'Peaceful Transition from Socialism to Capitalism?' (*Monthly Review*, March 1964).
14. G. B. Shaw, 'The Economic Basis of Socialism', in *Fabian Essays in Socialism*; ed. G. B. Shaw (Walter Scott, 1889), p. 22.
15. See, for example, D. Jay, *Socialism in the New Society* (Longmans, 1962).
16. F. Engels, *Anti-Dühring* (1878); reprinted in *Socialist Economics*, eds A. Nove and D. Nuti (Penguin Books, 1972), p. 24.
17. P. Slater, *The Pursuit of Loneliness* (Penguin Books, 1975).
18. J. K. Galbraith, *The Affluent Society* (Hamish Hamilton, 1958).
19. J. K. Galbraith, *The New Industrial State* (*op. cit.*).
20. A savage review of *The New Industrial State* appeared in *The Times Literary Supplement* of 23 November 1967. For a more moderate, though still critical review, see J. E. Meade, 'Is "The New Industrial State" Inevitable?', in *Economic Journal*, LXXVIII, June 1968.

3. PLANNING IN THE THIRTIES

1. R. H. S. Crossman, 'Towards a Philosophy of Socialism', in *New Fabian Essays* (*op. cit.*), p. 3.
2. N. Harris, *Competition and the Corporate State* (Methuen, 1972), p. 13.
3. T. F. Lindsay and M. Harrington, *The Conservative Party 1918–1970* (Macmillan, 1974), p. 4.

4. N. Harris, *Competition and the Corporate State* (*op. cit.*), p. 31.
5. *Ibid*, p. 48.
6. D. Winch, *Economics and Policy* (Hodder & Stoughton, 1969), p. 73.
7. E. F. Durbin, 'The Importance of Planning' (1935), in *Problems of Economic Planning* (Routledge & Kegan Paul, 1949), p. 42.
8. S. H. Beer, *Modern British Politics* (Faber 1969), Chapter X.
9. H. Macmillan, *Winds of Change* (Macmillan, 1966), p. 223.
10. R. Boothby, H. Macmillan, J. Loder and O. Stanley, *Industry and the State* (Macmillan, 1927), p. 41.
11. H. Macmillan, *The Middle Way* (Macmillan, 1938), p. 97.
12. C. R. Attlee, *The Labour Party in Perspective* (Gollancz, 1937), p. 284.
13. *Ibid*, p. 176.
14. G. D. H. Cole, *Plan for Democratic Britain* (Odhams Press, 1939), p. 25.
15. J. Strachey, *The Coming Struggle for Power* (Victor Gollancz, 1934), p. 113.
16. *Ibid*, p. 113.

4. THE POST-WAR LABOUR GOVERNMENT AND PLANNING

1. Cmd 7046, February 1947.
2. C. Cooke, *Life of Richard Stafford Cripps* (Hodder & Stoughton), p. 354.
3. *Idem*.
4. D. Jay, *Labour's Plan for 1947* (Labour Party, March 1947), p. 6.
5. H. Morrison, *Economic Planning* (Institute of Public Administration, 1946), p. 15.
6. E. A. G. Robinson, 'The Overall Allocation of Resources', in *Lessons of the British War Economy*;

ed. D. N. Chester (Cambridge University Press, 1951), p. 34.

7. British Labour's Reconstruction Programme, *The Old World and the New Society* (1943).

8. H. Morrison, *Economic Planning* (*op. cit.*).

9. B. Donoughue and G. W. Jones, *Herbert Morrison* (Weidenfeld & Nicholson, 1973).

10. *Ibid*, p. 354.

11. *Ibid*, p. 406.

12. J. C. R. Dow, *The Management of the British Economy 1945–60* (Cambridge University Press, 1964), p. 33.

13. Cmd 7344, March 1948.

14. European Cooperation. Memoranda submitted to OEEC relating to Economic Affairs in the period 1949 to 1953 (Cmnd 7572, December 1948).

15. E. A. G. Robinson, *Economic Planning in the United Kingdom, Some Lessons* (Cambridge University Press, 1967).

16. J. Mitchell, *Groundwork to Economic Planning* (*op. cit.*).

17. *Ibid*, p. 103.

18. *Ibid*, p. 119.

19. *Ibid*, p. 116.

20. Cmd 7647, March 1949.

21. Cmd 7915, March 1950.

22. Cmd 8195, April 1951.

23. S. H. Beer, *Modern British Politics* (*op. cit.*), p. 149.

24. *Ibid*, p. 152.

25. *Post-War Reconstruction*, Interim Report (TUC, 1944).

26. P. Addison, *The Road to 1945* (Jonathan Cape, 1975), p. 272.

27. R. H. S. Crossman, M. Foot and I. Mikardo, *Keep Left* (New Statesman Pamphlet, 1947).

28. M. Foot, *Aneurin Bevan*, Vol., 2, 1945–60 (Davis Poynter, 1973), p. 258.

29. *Ibid*, p. 286.

30. *Ibid*, p. 288.

31. *Ibid*, p. 336.

32. F. A. Hayek, *The Road to Serfdom* (Routledge & Kegan Paul, 1944). See also J. Jewkes, *The New Ordeal by Planning* (Macmillan, 1968); first published as *Ordeal by Planning* in 1948.

5. CONSERVATIVE PLANNING, 1961-4

1. T. Smith, 'Britain', in *Planning, Politics and Public Policy*; ed. J. Hayward and M. Watson (Cambridge University Press, 1975), p. 57.
2. H. Macmillan, *At the End of the Day* (Macmillan, 1973), p. 37.
3. *Ibid*, p. 398.
4. Cmnd 972, 1956.
5. J. C. R. Dow, *The Management of the British Economy 1945-60* (*op. cit.*), p. 399.
6. A brief account of indicative planning is provided in J. E. Meade, *The Intelligent Radical's Guide to Economic Policy* (Allen & Unwin, 1975).
7. *Ibid*, p. 106.
8. Political and Economic Planning, *Growth in the British Economy* (Allen & Unwin, 1960), p. 24.
9. *Ibid*, p. 221.
10. T. Wilson, *Planning and Growth* (Macmillan, 1964).
11. J. Leruez, *Economic Planning and Politics in Britain* (*op. cit.*), p. 87.
12. *Crossbow* 16 (1961), p. 6.
13. Lord Butler, *The Art of the Possible* (Hamish Hamilton, 1971), p. 146.
14. Conservative and Unionist Central Office, *The Industrial Charter* (1947).
15. J. Leruez, *Economic Planning and Politics in Britain* (*op. cit.*), p. 92.
16. H. C. Debates 645, Col. 220 (25 July 1961).
17. *Ibid*, Col. 439 (26 July 1961).
18. N. Harris, *Competition and the Corporate State* (*op. cit.*), p. 242.
19. S. Brittan, *Steering the Economy* (Penguin Books, 1971), pp. 241-3.

20. S. Blank, *Government and Industry in Britain* (Saxon House, 1973).
21. W. Grant and D. Marsh, *The Confederation of British Industry* (Hodder & Stoughton, 1977), Chapter 2.
22. Political and Economic Planning, *Growth in the British Economy* (*op. cit.*), p. 234.
23. J. Mitchell, *Groundwork to Economic Planning* (*op. cit.*), p. 143.
24. R. Bailey, *Managing the British Economy* (*op. cit.*), p. 38.

6. THE LABOUR PARTY AND THE NATIONAL
   PLAN, 1964-6

1. S. Brittan, *Steering the Economy* (*op. cit.*), p. 227.
2. A. A. Berle and G. C. Means, *The Modern Corporation and Private Property* (first published in 1932; revised edition, Harcourt, World & Brace, 1967).
3. J. Burnham, *The Managerial Revolution* (first published in 1941; Greenwood Press, 1972).
4. C. Kerr, J. T. Dunlop, F. H. Harbison and C. A. Myers, *Industrialism and Industrial Man* (Heinemann, 1962).
5. C. A. R. Crosland, 'The Transition from Capitalism', in *New Fabian Essays* (*op. cit.*), p. 45.
6. *Ibid*, p. 64.
7. C. A. R. Crosland, *The Future of Socialism* (Jonathan Cape, 1956), p. 500.
8. *Ibid*, p. 503.
9. M. Foot, *Aneurin Bevan*, Vol. 2 (*op. cit.*), pp. 646–67.
10. Labour Party, *Plan for Progress* (1958), p. 8.
11. H. Wilson, *The Labour Government 1964–70* (Weidenfeld & Nicholson and Michael Joseph, 1971), p. 3.
12. *Ibid*, p. 5.
13. Lord George-Brown, *In My Way* (Gollancz, 1971), p. 95.

14. R. Bailey, *Managing the Economy (op. cit.)*, p. 69.
15. *The National Plan* (Cmd 2764).
16. R. Bailey, *Managing the Economy (op. cit.)*, p. 75.
17. *Ibid*, p. 77.
18. R. G. Opie, 'Economic Planning and Growth', in *The Labour Government's Economic Record, 1964–70*; ed. W. Beckerman (Duckworth, 1972), p. 170.
19. S. Brittan, 'Inquest on Planning in Britain', in *Planning* XXXIII, 498 (January 1967), p. 3.
20. R. Lecomber, 'Government planning, with and without the cooperation of industry', in *Economics of Planning*, Vol. 10, 1–2 (1970).
21. R. G. Opie, 'Economic Planning and Growth' (*op. cit.*), p. 172.
22. J. Leruez, *Economic Planning and Politics in Britain (op. cit.)*, p. 179.
23. S. Brittan, 'Inquest on Planning in Britain' (*op. cit.*), p. 11.
24. A. Gamble, *The Conservative Nation* (Routledge & Kegan Paul, 1974).
25. Lord George-Brown, *In My Way (op. cit.)*, p. 119.
26. H. Wilson, *The Labour Government (op. cit.)*, p. 138.

7. THE AFTERMATH OF NATIONAL PLANNING

1. S. Brittan, 'Inquest on Planning in Britain' (*op. cit.*), p. 3.
2. Department of Economic Affairs, *The Task Ahead* (HMSO, 1969).
3. H.M. Treasury, *Economic Prospects to 1972 – a Revised Assessment* (HMSO, 1970).
4. Conservative Central Office, *A Better Tomorrow* (1970).
5. S. Holland, *The Socialist Challenge* (Quartet Books, 1975).
6. *Ibid*, p. 168.
7. *Ibid*, p. 188.

8. *Ibid*, p. 120.
9. Labour Party, *National Enterprise Board* (Opposition Green Paper, 1973).
10. *The Regeneration of British Industry* (Cmnd 5710, August 1974).

8. THE FUTURE OF PLANNING

1. *Trade and Industry*, 4 April 1975, p. 2.
2. F. W. Paish, 'Government Policy and Business Investment' in *How the Economy Works* (Macmillan, 1970), p. 104.
3. S. Holland, *The Socialist Challenge* (*op. cit.*), p. 207.
4. R. G. Opie, 'Economic Planning and Growth' (*op. cit.*), p. 172.
5. See, for example, Barrington Moore Jr, *Social Origins of Dictatorship and Democracy* (Beacon Press, 1967), chapter 2.
6. F. A. Hayek, *The Road to Serfdom* (*op. cit.*), p. 30.
7. C. E. Lindblom, 'The Sociology of Planning: Thought and Social Interaction' in *Economic Planning East and West*; ed., M. Bornstein (Ballinger, 1975).
8. *Ibid*, p. 44.

Select Bibliography

GENERAL

J. Leruez, *Economic Planning and Politics in Britain*; tr. M. Harrison (Martin Robertson, 1975)

Covers much the same ground as the present book, though it provides greater detail on regional planning, industrial policy and incomes policies. It has the merits and disadvantages of a French perspective: events are viewed with a cool eye, but Britain is only praised when it comes near to adopting the French style of planning.

D. Winch, *Economics and Policy* (Hodder & Stoughton, 1969)

A detailed study of the relationship between economic theory and economic policy.

THE PLANNING DEBATE

The Liberal pro-market case is presented in:

M. Friedman, *Capitalism and Freedom* (Macmillan, 1973)

F. A. Hayek, *The Road to Serfdom* (Routledge & Kegan Paul, 1944)

S. Brittan, *Capitalism and the Permissive Society* (Macmillan, 1973)

Specific attacks on planning from the liberal side are presented in:

J. Jewkes, *The New Ordeal by Planning* (Macmillan, 1968)

D. S. Lees, *Uses and Abuses of National Planning* (University College of Swansea, 1966)

The Lib-Lab view (held by those who support the objectives of the Labour Party yet emphasize the use of market processes) is presented in:

A. Lewis, *The Principles of Economic Planning* (Allen & Unwin, 3rd edition 1969)

Select Bibliography

J. E. Meade, *The Intelligent Radical's Guide to Economic Policy* (Allen & Unwin, 1975)

The case for planning is presented in:

T. Balogh, *Planning for Progress* (Fabian Tract 346, 1963)

M. Stewart, 'Planning and Persuasion in a Mixed Economy' (*Political Quarterly*, April–June 1964)

POST-WAR POLITICS

P. Addison, *The Road to 1945* (Jonathan Cape, 1975)
An excellent account of the first post-war Labour Government and the development of its policies during the war.

S. H. Beer, *Modern British Politics* (Faber, 1969)
A stimulating view of the Conservative and Labour Parties' history.

C. A. R. Crosland, *The Future of Socialism* (Jonathan Cape, 1956)
The key statement of the 'revisionist' case in the Labour Party.

A. Bevan, *In Place of Fear* (MacGibbon & Kee, new edition 1961)
Planning was Bevan's 'King Charles's head'. Chapter 9 specifically attacks economic individualism.

S. Holland, *The Socialist Challenge* (Quartet Books, 1975)
The theoretical base for the Labour Party NEC's calls for planning and extended public ownership.

POST-WAR ECONOMIC PLANNING

S. Brittan, *Steering the Economy* (Penguin Books, 1971)
The best account of the period, with particular reference to the Treasury.

J. C. R. Dow, *The Management of the British Economy 1945–60* (Cambridge University Press, 1964)

Classic study of the post-war years. The first attempt at a detailed appraisal of demand management.

THE POST-WAR HISTORY OF PLANNING

J. Mitchell, *Groundwork to Economic Planning* (Secker & Warburg, 1966)
Covers the period from the end of the war with a full description of the Long-term Programme. Written in 1965, the book seems in retrospect far too optimistic about the DEA experiment.
R. Bailey, *Managing the British Economy* (Hutchinson, 1968)
An insider's view of NEDO by a former director of Political and Economic Planning.
S. Brittan, 'Inquest on Planning in Britain' (*Planning* XXXIII, 498, January 1967)
A devastating analysis of the defects of *The National Plan*. One cannot now be so confident that the failure to devalue was a major cause of the plan's collapse.

OFFICIAL DOCUMENTS

The Long-term Programme of 1948 was officially known as 'European Cooperation. Memoranda submitted to OEEC relating to Economic Affairs in the period 1949 to 1953' (Cmnd 7572, 1948)
NEDC, *The Growth of the United Kingdom Economy to 1966* (HMSO, 1963)
NEDC, *Conditions Favourable to Faster Growth* (HMSO, 1963)
The National Plan (Cmnd 2764, 1965)
DEA, *The Task Ahead, Economic Assessment to 1972* (HMSO, 1969)
The Regeneration of British Industry (Cmd 5710, 1974)

INDEX

Index

169

Keynes

D. E. Moggridge

An outstanding account of Keynes's intellectual origins and characteristic modes of thought which sets in broader perspective his contributions to the formulations of British economic policy and the development of economic theory between 1913 and 1946.

Drawing on his unique knowledge of Keynes's writings, published and unpublished, Professor Moggridge provides the most complete account of the emergence of Keynes's masterpieces, *Economic Consequence of the Peace* (1918), *A Treatise on Money* (1930), and *The General Theory of Employment, Interest and Money* (1936).

'. . . the best book that I have yet met about Keynes as a person, his intellectual background and preconceptions.'

Sir Austin Robinson

'. . . not only succeeds in saying something new but even succeeds in saying the old better than it has ever been said before.'

Professor Mark Blaug

'Within its short compass, the book manages to be balanced, authoritative, and non-polemical – a welcome change from many of the attempts that have been made to assess Keynes's contribution since his death.'   Professor Donald Winch

The Fontana Economic History of Europe

General Editor: Carlo M. Cipolla, Professor of Economic History at the Universities of Pavia and California, Berkeley.

'There can be no doubt that these volumes make an extremely significant addition to the literature of European economic history, where the need for new large comparative works has long been felt . . . It is overall a project of vision and enormous value.'

Times Literary Supplement

1. The Middle Ages

Contributors: Cipolla: J. C. Russell: Jacques Le Goff: Richard Roehl: Lynn White Jr.: Georges Duby: Sylvia Thrupp: Jacques Bernard: Edward Miller.

2. The Sixteenth and Seventeenth Centuries

Contributors: Cipolla: Roger Mols: Walter Minchinton: Hermann Kellenbenz: Aldo de Maddalena: Domenico Sella: Kristof Glamann: Geoffrey Parker.

3. The Industrial Revolution

Contributors: André Armengaud: Walter Minchinton: Samuel Lilley: Gertrand Gille: Barry Supple: R. M. Hartwell: J. F. Bergier: Paul Bairoch: Donald Winch: M. J. T. Lewis.

4. The Emergence of Industrial Societies

Part 1: Contributors: Claude Fohlen: Knut Borchardt: Phyllis Deane: N. T. Gross: Luciano Cafagna: Jan Dhondt & Marinette Bruwier.
Part 2: Contributors: Lennart Jörberg: Gregory Crossman: Jordi Nadal: B. M. Biucchi: William Woodruff: B. R. Mitchell.

5. The Twentieth Century

Part 1: Contributors: Milos Macura: A. S. Deaton: Walter Galenson: Giorgio Pellicelli: Roy and Kay MacLeod: Georges Brondel: Robert Campbell.
Part 2: Contributors: Hermann Priebe: Angus Maddison: Carlo Zacchia: Fred Hirsch and Peter Oppenheimer: Benjamin Ward: Max Nicholson.

6. Contemporary Economics

Part 1: Contributors: Johan de Vries: Claude Fohlen: A. J. Youngson: Karl Hardach: Sergio Ricossa: John Pinder.
Part 2: Contributors: Lennart Jörberg: and Olle Krantz: Josep Fontana and Jordi Nadal: Hansjörg Siegenthaler: Alfred Zauberman: B. R. Mitchell.

Fontana Books

Fontana is a leading paperback publisher of fiction and non-fiction, with authors ranging from Alistair MacLean, Agatha Christie and Desmond Bagley to Solzhenitsyn and Pasternak, from Gerald Durrell and Joy Adamson to the famous Modern Masters series.

In addition to a wide-ranging collection of internationally popular writers of fiction, Fontana also has an outstanding reputation for history, natural history, military history, psychology, psychiatry, politics, economics, religion and the social sciences.

All Fontana books are available at your bookshop or newsagent; or can be ordered direct. Just fill in the form and list the titles you want.

FONTANA BOOKS, Cash Sales Department, G.P.O. Box 29, Douglas, Isle of Man, British Isles. Please send purchase price, plus 8p per book. Customers outside the U.K. send purchase price, plus 10p per book. Cheque, postal or money order. No currency.

NAME (Block letters)

ADDRESS
